Curriculum Leadership

Curriculum Leadership

Beyond Boilerplate Standards

Second Edition

Leo H. Bradley, Shirley A. Curtis,
Thomas A. Kessinger, and
D. Mark Meyers

ROWMAN & LITTLEFIELD
Lanham • Boulder • New York • London

Published by Rowman & Littlefield
A wholly owned subsidiary of The Rowman & Littlefield Publishing Group, Inc.
4501 Forbes Boulevard, Suite 200, Lanham, Maryland 20706
www.rowman.com

Unit A, Whitacre Mews, 26–34 Stannary Street, London SE11 4AB

British Library Cataloguing in Publication Information Available

Library of Congress Cataloging-in-Publication Data Available
ISBN: 978-1-4758-4007-0 (cloth : alk. paper)
ISBN: 978-1-4758-4008-7 (pbk. : alk. paper)
ISBN: 978-1-4758-4009-4 (electronic)

To Jacob, Sarah, Serena, and Sophia

Take your stands, make your mark.

Never forget that the only failure is the failure to try.

To my children and grandchildren

Only two things happen in life—

good things and learning experiences.

Be kind, take risk, and live life to the fullest.

For William, Samuel, and Mary Grace

Contents

Preface

Curriculum Leadership: Beyond Boilerplate Standards is designed to be a tool to create and continuously improve curriculum. The book is meant to engage the reader in reflection and subsequent action during the entire curriculum process, from design to evaluation. Throughout the book, the significance of leadership regarding the quality of curriculum is a theme. Chapter 1, "Philosophy, an Overview," begins the work with a discussion of the philosophical foundations that underpin the study and application of leadership. Chapter 2, "Curriculum Leadership: The Unique Educational Leadership Domain," explains how all the processes are affected by leadership. Please note that the term *leadership* is used instead of leader.

Leadership for curriculum program development and implementation is found throughout the hierarchy of the school. Sometimes the leadership comes from the administration; in other instances, faculty members provide it. Many different organizational structures are used in schools to manage the curriculum program. Therefore, the leadership does not always depend on the organizational position held by the educator but rather on the expertise required to accomplish curriculum improvement. However, regardless of the formal position of the person in the hierarchical structure, the leadership principles advocated in this book universally apply. The cognitive and affective skills and concepts that make up effective curriculum are based on servitor leadership principles rather than authority. The power of servitor leadership exists throughout the school organization. Wherever that power is located, that is where the leadership will be.

The presentation of the material in this book is not rhetorical. In some instances, advocacy in specific processes or decisions, such as how to select participants for curriculum, is easily discernible. However, the intent of the text is to present the processes, decisions, and tasks in such a way that the readers may determine for themselves whether to proceed as suggested by the author, or to make adaptations.

The book is laid out in the order that curriculum work takes place. Chapter 3, "Principles and Operational Definitions of Curriculum," presents the foundations and operational definitions that serve as the basis for the curriculum process. The foundation principles discussed show how to connect the curriculum with the mission of the school. This is the chapter that clearly delineates how theory and practice come together. The operational definitions clarify exactly what the various curricular terms mean within the contexts of this book. Hopefully, the discussion will contribute to the effort within the field to eliminate many of the ambiguities that plague the curriculum field. At the very least it will focus the readers on understanding the application of the terminology.

Chapter 4, "Curriculum Development Process," presents the processes of curriculum design and development. This is the heart of curriculum. It is in this phase that the organizational ownership and responsiveness necessary for effective implementation will be either won or lost. The strategies presented in this chapter are designed around producing one outcome: ownership and responsiveness by the principals and teachers who are charged with implementing the curriculum. Without that ownership and responsiveness, the curriculum program is doomed to failure. With it, the continual improvement of student learning, and thus successful school reform, can occur.

Involvement in curriculum decision making is a prerequisite to creating teacher and principal ownership and responsiveness to curriculum. It deserves a chapter of its own. In chapter 5, "Curriculum Decision Making," emphasis is placed on using consensus and ensuring that curriculum maintains a status commensurate with its significance in the accomplishment of student learning.

Chapter 6, "Curriculum Documents," discusses document evaluation, both format and content. Effective curriculum documents have a format that makes them feasible and easy for teachers to use. Content evaluation deals with the validity of learning objectives and an assessment of the congruency among curriculum, instruction, and assessment/testing. The document evaluation process presented can be used for both printed documents and curriculum information stored by technology. The evaluation of documents is looked at separately from program evaluation. This approach is taken because effective documents are viewed as a part of the design and development process.

Chapter 7, "Curriculum Program Evaluation," is devoted to curriculum program evaluation—an absolute necessity in order for curriculum to optimize learning and stand the test of accountability, both within and outside the system. Therefore, summative program evaluation, centering on student learning, is presented. In addition, to best serve the needs and expectations of a continuous improvement school, formative evaluation tools are explained and tied to specific aims of the curriculum program.

One aspect of curriculum design and development that is consistent is the presence of planned change. Chapter 8, "The Role of Paradigms in Curriculum Change," looks at curriculum paradigms that best serve schools pursuing continuous curriculum improvement.

Throughout the book, the opinion that curriculum design and instruction must be congruent for a successful educational program is repeated. It is thus fitting that chapter 9 of the book, "Correlating Curriculum Design with How the Brain Learns," presents instructional research-based strategies and activities that will deliver the planned curriculum in such a way as to promote student learning and retention. It can be argued that this chapter is totally instructional in nature and, therefore, out of place in a curriculum design and development book. The philosophical position of this text is that since the purpose of curriculum is the improvement of student learning, this purpose cannot be fulfilled unless there is attention to the instructional program as it relates to curriculum, and a correlation between the two. Therefore, chapter 10 discusses the instructional component. To not do so would negate the entire thesis of the book that neither curriculum nor instruction should stand alone—that they are, by their very nature, interrelated. The purpose of this book is to show how that interrelationship can be maximized for the continuous improvement of learning.

Technology has increased the efficiency of the curriculum development process and significantly altered instruction. With the effective use of technology, curriculum development as an ongoing process is feasible and can replace time lines that formerly drove periodic curriculum revision by subject area. Chapter 10, "Technology and Curriculum Development," looks at technology and curriculum development and the power afforded by the application of the technology mind-set, rather than simply focusing on the use of technology in conjunction with curriculum development.

Chapter 11, "Student Credentialing," describes how student credentialing can be used as an authentic measurement of student achievement beyond boilerplate standards. This multifactored assessment is an accountability process that verifies the skills and knowledge each student has demonstrated in preparing for the next transition level. Student credentialing is more specific than letter grades or a composite score on a standardized test. It has the potential to make schools accountable for all student achievement, not just boilerplate standards.

Acknowledgments

This book is a true collaboration of the four of us, Leo H. Bradley, Shirley A. Curtis, Thomas A. Kessinger, and D. Mark Meyers. Collectively, we bring a theoretical perspective and experience to the field of curriculum, including philosophical foundations, curriculum process, leadership, assessment, and technology. We have incorporated the many good practices that we have participated in and observed in schools with expertise in how to plan, implement, and evaluate a comprehensive curriculum program that aims higher than boilerplate standards. Taken collectively, they have formed the basis for this text.

Introduction

Any book on school curriculum and instruction should begin by anticipating and meeting the needs and expectations of its key players. The overriding learning and teaching need and expectation today is knowledge. We are in the information age. In the nineteenth and twentieth centuries, the United States has moved from an agricultural to blue-collar industry to a knowledge-based economy. What school curriculum and instruction must do to anticipate, meet, and exceed the needs and expectations of its key players in the twenty-first century is to teach students the knowledge and skills they need to know and what they can do with what they have learned.

In 1996 the definition of the term *basic skills* was found in the book *Teaching the New Basic Skills: Principles for Educating Children to Thrive in a Changing Economy*, by Richard J. Murname and Frank Levy.[1] The basic skills were as follows:

- The traditional cognitive skills, reading, writing, math, social studies, science, problem solving, and so forth performed at a competence level higher than many high school graduates now attain.
- Work in groups with persons of diverse backgrounds.
- Make effective oral and written presentations.
- Use personal computers to carry out simple tasks like word processing.

"But the world in which schools operate today is very different from the one of just a few years ago—and all signs point to more change ahead. The global economy is transforming jobs and the 21st century workplace for which schools prepare students"[2] (NPBEA, 2015). For students to survive in a complex, ever-changing, digital, global environment, they not only need traditional cognitive skills but higher order thinking, deeper understanding, information and communication technology, and life and career skills.

Curriculum and instruction must be built around the educational mission, which, like basic skills, has undergone change. Traced historically, the educational mission for schools was, at first, schooling for some, albeit for differing purposes. Then the mission moved to compulsory schooling for all; learning for some and training for others. Today the mission is compulsory learning for all. The movement from compulsory attendance to compulsory learning has moved the schools and their staffs to a position of public accountability.

Interestingly, the accountability movement led by the political structure of the society has not been accompanied by a change in the basic conditions under which schools organize or operate. The body politic tends to view education as a totally rational institution, with complete control of all the variables that affect student success. In fact, schools contain elements of a nonrational institution, meaning that stakeholders not within the control of schools, significantly affect student achievement. Therefore, curriculum and instructional improvement must be accomplished by the interdependent work of educators and the other stakeholders who impact the system. Reform based on only a few of the stakeholders will not have a positive impact. Perhaps, it will have no impact at all. The mission must be pursued by all the stakeholders through a systematic process.

In the past, curriculum planning usually began from the bottom up: primary, intermediate, middle school, high school, continuing education. Curriculum planning needs to begin with the end in mind. The guiding question is: What do the students need to know when they leave us? Curriculum goals, programs, courses, and assessment systems should reflect this question.

Curriculum planning should also be based on the question: What do people want from schools?

Based on the work by Partnerships for 21st Century Learning—a national nonprofit organization of education-related organizations, business partners, and government leaders—skills essential to student success have expanded to include the following:

• Mastery of the key subjects, English, reading or language arts, world languages, arts, mathematics, economics, science, geography, history, government and civics; in addition, schools must promote an understanding of academic content at much higher levels
• Learning and innovation skills of collaboration, communication, creativity and innovation, critical thinking and problem solving
• Information, media, and technology skills
• Life and career skills[3]

The answers to these two questions—(a) what do students need to know when they leave us and (b) what do people want from schools—form the basis for curriculum design, development, implementation, and evaluation. This book assumes that posture and attempts to present activities and decisions in such a way that these two questions permeate the entire process.

NOTES

1. Richard J. Mumame and Frank Levy, *Teaching the New Basic Skills: Principles for Educating Children to Thrive in a Changing Economy* (New York: Free Press, 1996), 9.

2. National Policy Board for Educational Administration (NPBEA), *Professional Standards for Educational Leaders 2015* (Reston, VA: Author, 2015).

3. Partnership for 21st Learning, *Framework for 21st Century Learning* (2017). http://www.p21.org/storage/documents/docs/P21_framework_0816.pdf (accessed November 6, 2017).

Chapter 1

Philosophy

An Overview

INTRODUCTION

According to George Knight—who borrowed the term from Charles Silber-man, "Mindlessness is the most pertinent and accurate criticism of American education" (Knight, 2008, p. 3). Essentially, educators have been more concerned with motion rather than with progress, that is, with means more than ends. As a result, they have failed to raise the bigger question of purpose in education; instead their focus has been on methodology. Indeed, the cart should be methodology, and, more importantly, the horse is purpose.

What education needs today is a clear vision of "why all this education" and "for/to what purpose" (Knight, 2008, p. 4). To obtain this vision, one needs to ask the fundamental questions that are encased in a study of philosophy: questions about reality (metaphysics), knowledge or truth (epistemology), and values (axiology). Without this awareness of the major dimensions of philosophy—especially as applied to education—"mindlessness" will prevail.

Every teacher or educator has a philosophy of life that one carries into the classroom. This means each one has notions about the world, the meaning of life, and what is both morally and ethically right. From this comes a philosophy of education that is exhibited each day. Knight reminds and encourages us as follows:

> To say that each of us has a philosophy of education and life that we daily act upon does not mean that we have a good (or bad) philosophy, or even a philosophy that we have thought through. Our philosophy may exist at the subliminal level. The plea . . . is that all educators need a consciously examined and thoroughly considered philosophy of education if they are to make the most efficient use of both their own time and their students' energy. (Knight, 2008, p. 160)

When one does this, then an educator is better (read consciously) prepared to consider key educational issues and practices.

Today, for many reasons, many educators see a close correlation between curriculum, methods, and assessment. At times this scheme is depicted in the form of a three-legged stool or an equilateral triangle, denoting the importance of and emphasis on each leg or side. Curriculum includes content, standards, and essentially "the what" of teaching and learning. Methods, techniques, and strategies form the essence of pedagogy; these methods consider "the how" and "the why." Assessment is evaluation or measurement; it investigates "to what degree" something has occurred either in a formative or summative fashion. Each one of these three components must be connected— that is aligned—to an overarching whole or there is an imbalance present.

When a teacher or educator embarks on a study, review, or application of curriculum, the lenses worn should be realized. Why? The preferred lens will lead one to naturally follow a particular curricular and instructional path that has a history and undoubtedly a philosophical basis connected to it. Indeed, it is important for educational practitioners to know and to implement a desired or preferred curriculum. Such a focus helps in avoiding "mindlessness" that again is frequently found in education today.

CURRENT PHILOSOPHIES AND EDUCATIONAL THEORIES

The chief philosophies of education that one could/should examine in the twenty-first century include the following four prominent theories: progressivism, perennialism, essentialism or neo-essentialism, and behaviorism. Each one is grounded in at least one major philosophy or way of thinking about life, and some of these theories incorporate more than one way of thinking or highlights an important focus. Therefore, it is relevant to review each of these theories because the theory embraced will ultimately result in a given set of educational practices that consider the social function of schools, the nature of the student, the role of the teacher, particular teaching methods, and particular curricular designs and emphases (Knight, 2008, p. 35).

PROGRESSIVISM

Progressivism is a late nineteenth, early twentieth-century educational theory that was founded or best articulated by John Dewey, who at times is referred to as the "father of progressivism." Dewey was influenced by major philosophers (G.W.F. Hegel), psychologists (William James and Charles Peirce), and scientists/writers (Charles Darwin). As a result, he became an advocate of pragmatism that serves as the major grounding of progressive educational thought.

Pragmatism, as a philosophical base, was critical of the older or earlier systems of philosophy (namely idealism, realism, and theistic realism or neo-Scholasticism), which pragmatists say made the mistake of looking for absolutes, universals, or eternals in reality (metaphysics). Pragmatists focused on change (i.e., they viewed the world as a changing entity with its myriad problems) and on the empirical sciences. In other words, pragmatism stresses knowledge or truth (epistemology), not metaphysics, and this knowledge is rooted in experience. Thus, pragmatists assert that individuals do not simply receive knowledge; they make it as they interact with or experience an environment (Dewey, 1938). To a pragmatist, truth is what works. From this base, comes progressivism. "Pragmatism, therefore, may be seen as a central influence in progressive educational theory" (Knight, 2008, p. 102).

Progressive education was a part of a larger political-social movement of general reform that characterized life in the United States in the late nineteenth and the early twentieth centuries as the country tried to adjust to the three major issues of immigration, urbanization, and industrialization. This educational theory began as a definite reaction against traditional education ways such as formal methods of instruction, authoritarian teaching, and rote learning. To progressive educators, education is not a preparation for life but rather life itself, and thus should represent life as authentically as possible.

There is no central dogma to progressivism, but there are some major tenets that most progressive educators espouse. Some progressive principles include the following: (1) the focus should be on the child, and the child should be able to develop naturally; (2) interest is the best stimulus; (3) the teacher is a resource, guide, and facilitator; (4) school should be a lab that encourages cooperation and democratic ways; and (5) close cooperation should exist between school and home. In addition, the aim of progressive education is to educate the individual according to their interests and needs, but this assumes the child knows the basics; the curriculum centers on activities and projects (see William H. Kilpatrick for details on the method); and the educational implications include instruction that features problem solving and group activities.

A more recent contributor to and disciple of progressive education is Theodore R. Sizer (and his wife, Nancy). In 1984, Sizer, a professor of education at Brown University, and several of his colleagues published results from "A Study of High Schools," a five-year investigation of teaching and learning that found that American high schools generally were remarkably similar and quite inadequate. Sizer's contribution, *Horace's Compromise: The Dilemma of the American High School*—and two subsequent works comprising a trilogy—considered how schools might be designed more wisely. From this evolved a set of beliefs about the purpose and practice of schooling that formed Sizer's Coalition of Essential Schools' (CES) ten common principles:

- Learning to use one's mind well
- Less is more, depth over breath in curriculum coverage
- Goals apply to all students
- Personalization
- Student-as-worker, teacher-as-coach
- Demonstration of mastery
- A tone of decency and trust
- Commitment to the entire school
- Resources dedicated to teaching and learning
- Democracy and equity

(Refer to the CES website for more information; Davidson, 2010, pp. 170–171)

Finally, since there is no central dogma to progressive education today, there are many branches of progressive education that include humanism, social reconstructionism, constructivism (in part), futurism, critical pedagogy, and deschooling. Each of these subtypes has its own points of emphasis that will impact curricular design.

PERENNIALISM

Perennialism, another educational theory, is frequently depicted as a major reaction to progressive education. It first appeared during the 1930s at the University of Chicago. This theory is directly rooted in neo-Scholasticism and indirectly in idealism and realism. Some major proponents of perennialism were Robert. M. Hutchins (a former president at the University of Chicago), Mortimer Adler, Jacques Maritain, and Allan Bloom.

Some major principles of perennialism are as follows: (1) people are rational animals; (2) human nature is universally consistent, and therefore, education should be universally consistent; (3) knowledge is universally consistent, and, as a result, there are certain basic subjects that should be taught to all people; (4) the subject matter, not the child, should stand at the center of the educational endeavor; (5) the great works of the past—found especially in Western literature and history—are a repository of knowledge and wisdom that has stood the test of time and is still quite relevant today; and (6) education is a preparation for life, not life itself. Furthermore, the aim here is to educate the rational person (read the intellect); relative to curriculum, the subject matter is hierarchically arranged to cultivate the intellect; and a major implication is to focus on enduring human concerns as revealed in the great works or books of the West.

Robert Hutchins and Mortimer Adler assembled the list of the Great Books that are still present in many educational and community settings today. Adler (1982) also led the effort to reform K–12 education by way of *The Paideia Proposal* that highlighted the same objectives and course of study for all students. Today there are numerous examples of Paideia schools that span grades K–8 and K–12 institutions.

ESSENTIALISM

This is also an educational theory that first appears during the 1930s in the United States. Essentialism emphasizes the basics, that is, subjects, disciplines, or skills, found in the content of education. It is rooted or grounded in the ancient philosophical orientations of idealism and realism. Essentialism focuses on or adheres to the major idea that there are core (essential) subjects or disciplines that should be studied, and the teacher is the primary authority in the classroom.

The aim of essentialism is to educate a useful and competent individual. Its content includes the three Rs, liberal arts and science, academic disciplines, and academic excellence, and basic skills. Testing is approved for determining mastery of these subjects along with support for vigorous national standards. The essentialist tradition maintains that there are concerned citizens who believe the public schools have declined and that they need to return to stricter discipline and to a study of the "basics." Since the 1930s, the essentialists have advanced efforts to warn the American public of progressive notions (e.g., "life-adjustment education" and child-centered education) and the continuing erosion of education or learning in the United States (Kessinger, 2010).

Proponents of essentialism have included William C. Bagley, Isaac L. Kandel, Arthur Bestor, Admiral Hyman Rickover, James Bryant Conant, E. D. Hirsch Jr., Diane Ravitch, and various levels of government in the United States.

According to Ravitch (as noted by Gutek [2009]]), "The term essentialism is attributed to Michael Demiashkevich, who contrasted two competing theories, essentialism and individual-pragmatism, or progressivism in his *Introduction to the Philosophy of Education* (1935)." In 1938 a group of prominent educators led by William C. Bagley (1874–1946) began a movement that called for intellectual training in schools instead of "child growth and development." In *An Essentialist's Platform for the Advancement of American Education* (1938), Bagley stated that education requires hard work and attention as well as respect for genuine authority. He stressed the logical sequence of subjects and called for a "back to basics" movement to combat the lowering of academic standards. His disciples argued that progressive educational tendencies and practices were too soft and placed less emphasis on dealing with educational basics such as mastery of the three Rs and established facts.

During the 1950s, essentialists returned in force and again exerted antiprogressive sentiments via the Council for Basic Education under the leadership of Arthur Bestor and others. Bestor wrote *Educational Wastelands: The Retreat from Learning in our Public Schools*—a work that is also considered an essentialist manifesto. Joining Bestor in the attack on progressive ideas in public schools was Admiral Hyman G. Rickover, who deplored the lack of developed minds in the United States. He favored a European-type of education that focused on the basics and would lead students to be better prepared to enter an intensive and rigorous professional or technological program of study. With greater emphasis on the basics, many believed schools in the United States could produce the kinds of minds capable of matching those of the Soviets who had launched Sputnik in 1957. As a result of this event and these educational concerns, the federal government passed the National Defense Education Act in 1958.

The watershed event that brought the national government into the arena of public education in the United States was the issuance of A Nation at Risk (1983). This seminal government report—based on a study conducted at the direction of the president—noted that the "Federal Government has the primary responsibility to identify the national interest in education" (ANAR, 1983, p. 33). The report warned "the educational foundations of our society are presently being eroded by a rising tide of mediocrity that threatens our very future as a Nation and a people." Essentialists believe the essentials or core of education should be the "basics" of education. This report encouraged reform and suggested both higher standards and improved content. It called for a renewed emphasis or a neo-essentialist perspective on the "Five New Basics" that would include as a minimum standard for high school graduation: four years of English, three years each of mathematics, science, and social studies, and one-half year of computer science. In addition, two years of a foreign language were recommended for the college-bound student. In effect, this neo-essentialist movement that began in the 1980s revisited the ideas of the earlier essentialist movements and advocates of this position are frequently associated with political and cultural conservatives.

The recent legislations of No Child Left Behind (2001), The Race to the Top (2009), and Every Student Succeeds Act (2015) have continued the impetus for reform by the federal government. Indeed, the national government has increased its requirements on the states and, therefore, has continued its role as a dominant influence on public education. As a result of these laws, states are obligated to increase standards, insure achievement by means of tests, expect highly qualified teachers, and give evidence of greater accountability. These requirements are essentialist in design.

BEHAVIORISM

Another force in education since the middle of the twentieth century is behaviorism. This theory of education is rooted in realism (with an emphasis on natural laws), positivism, and materialism. Some proponents of behaviorism were Auguste Comte, Ivan Pavlov, John B. Watson, and B. F. Skinner. Comte sought to attain "positive" knowledge or that which can be verified empirically; in other words, the focus is on the observable and measurable. Watson is frequently referred to as the "father of modern behaviorism." Skinner, who authored *Beyond Freedom and Dignity,* was perhaps the most influential behaviorist of the twentieth century.

Behaviorism began to be applied to education in the 1950s, both to help understand student learning and to guide teaching. According to Drasgow (2010), the application of behaviorism to education was based on using principles that had been developed in the laboratory and on improving and thus reforming the educational system (Drasgow, 2010, p. 87).

Four major principles of behaviorism are as follows: (1) human beings are highly developed animals who learn in the same way that other animals learn; (2) education is a process of behavioral engineering; (3) the teacher's role is to create an effective learning environment; and (4) efficiency, economy, precision, and objectivity are central aspects of value in education (Knight, 2008).

An offshoot of behaviorism as well as progressivism is constructivism. Vygotsky's work, *The Mind in Society* (1938), is often cited as major treatise for this way of thinking. According to Kinnucan-Welsch (2010),

> Constructivism is a theory of knowing, with roots in psychology, philosophy and biology. It was introduced as a theory into a Western world dominated by a Western philosophical tradition including the foundation of realism which promulgated a theory of knowledge in which true knowledge represents an objective reality independent of observers of that reality and that individuals seek knowledge through a representation of that objective reality. (p. 215)

Constructivism, as a theory of learning, has played an important role in educational reform, both in terms of how instruction is designed and implemented in schools and classrooms and in terms of educator preparation.

CONCLUSION OR NEXT STEPS

Reflecting on the above four educational theories, one theory may relate or have greater relevancy to a given teacher, school, or school district in terms of its mission, vision, and available resources than the others. For this, the individual teacher and administrator (or leadership team) need to understand this as a given.

The key, though, decisions are made, and next steps considered are to avoid "mindlessness" and to develop a curriculum design or pattern or way of operating that is both consistent and meets the needs of a particular school or school district.

REFERENCES

Adler, M. (1982). *The paideia proposal: An educational manifesto.* New York: Macmillan Publishing Co., Inc.

Bagley, W. C. (2006). An essentialist's platform for the advancement of American education. In J. W. Null & D. Ravitch (Eds.), *Forgotten heroes of American education: The great tradition of teaching teachers.* Greenwich, CT: Information Age Publishing.

Bestor, A. E. (1953). *Educational wastelands: The retreat from learning in our public schools.* Urbana: University of Illinois Press.

Coalition of Essential Schools (CES). (2017). Retrieved from http://www.essential schools.org (accessed October 26, 2017).

Counts, G. (1932; renewed 1959). *Dare the school build a new social order?* Carbondale: Southern Illinois University Press.

Davidson, J. (2010). Coalition of Essential Schools. In T. C. Hunt, J. C. Carper, T. J. Lasley, & C. D. Raisch (Eds.), *Encyclopedia of educational reform and dissent* (vol. 1), pp. 170–171. Thousand Oaks, CA: SAGE Publications, Inc.

Dewey, J. (1916, renewed 1944, paperback edition 1966). *Democracy and education.* New York: The Free Press.

Dewey, J. (1938). *Experience and education: The Kappa Delta Pi Lecture Series.* New York: The Macmillan Company.

Drasgow, E. (2010). Behaviorism. In T. C. Hunt, J. C. Carper, T. J. Lasley, & C. D. Raisch (Eds.), *Encyclopedia of educational reform and dissent* (vol. 1), pp. 87–91. Thousand Oaks, CA: SAGE Publications, Inc.

Gutek, G. L. (2004). *Philosophical and ideological voices in education.* Boston: Pearson Education, Inc.

Gutek, G. L. (2009). *New perspectives on philosophy and education.* Upper Saddle River, NJ: Pearson Education, Inc.

Honderich, T. (Ed.). (2005). *The Oxford guide to philosophy.* New York: Oxford University Press, Inc.

Kessinger, T. (2010). Essentialism. In T. C. Hunt, J. C. Carper, T. J. Lasley, & C. D. Raisch (Eds.), *Encyclopedia of educational reform and dissent* (vol. 1), pp. 352–353. Thousand Oaks, CA: SAGE Publications, Inc.

Kilpatrick, T. (1918). The Project Method. In Teachers College Record 19 (September 1918), pp. 319–334. Retrieved from http://history matters.gmu.edu/d/4954/ (accessed October 26 and November 6, 2017).

Kinnucan-Welsch, K. (2010). Constructivism. In T. C. Hunt, J. C. Carper, T. J. Lasley, & C. D. Raisch (Eds.), *Encyclopedia of educational reform and dissent* (vol. 1), pp. 215–218. Thousand Oaks, CA: SAGE Publications, Inc.

Klein, A. (2017). The Every Student Succeeds Act: An ESSA Overview. https://www.edweek.org/ew/issues/every-student-succeeds-act/ (accessed October 26 and November 6, 2017).

Knight, G. (2008). *Issues and alternatives in educational philosophy* (4th ed.). Berrien Springs, MI: Andrews University Press.

National Commission on Excellence in Education. (1983). *A nation at risk: The imperative for educational reform*. Washington, D.C.: U.S. Department of Education. See also A Nation at Risk at https://www2.ed.gov/pubs/NatAtRisk/risk.html (accessed initially in April 1983 and on November 6, 2017 [archived]).

Noddings, N. (2016). *Philosophy of education* (4th ed.). Boulder, CO: Westview Press.

Ravitch, D. (2000). *Left back: A century of failed school reforms*. New York: Simon and Schuster.

Rury, J. (2013). *Education and social change: Contours in the history of American schooling* (4th ed.). New York: Routledge.

Sizer, T. (1985). *Horace's compromise: The dilemma of the American high school.* Boston: Houghton Mifflin Company.

Skinner, B. F. (1971). *Beyond freedom and dignity*. New York: Knopf.

Skinner, B. F. (1974). *About behaviorism*. New York: Knopf.

Vygotsky, L. S. (1938). *Mind in society: The development of higher psychological processes*. Cambridge, MA: Harvard University Press.

Watson, J. (1924). *Behaviorism*. New York: Norton.

Watras, J. (2008). *A history of American education*. New York: Pearson.

Chapter 2

Curriculum Leadership

The Unique Educational Leadership Domain

DEFINING CURRICULUM LEADER

The term *curriculum leader* is harder to define than other educational leadership positions such as superintendent or principal. In fact, it is not always defined by one's position. There are times when superintendents, principals, central office administrators, or teachers may be thrust into the role of curriculum leader. Curriculum leadership is often a role within a broader administrative position, as opposed to a position unto itself.

In other instances, the school system may have an administrative position that clearly assigns the role of curriculum leader to a specific person or position. The titles vary. The most common titles are curriculum director, curriculum specialist, curriculum coordinator, curriculum facilitator, or assistant superintendent for curriculum.

The need for curriculum leadership creates two possible scenarios. Either there is a position designated for the role, or the role is assumed by administrators or teachers for a portion of their administrative duties. Regardless of which situation is present, the principles of curriculum leadership described in this book apply. If a curriculum position is present, the person who occupies that position should follow the principles outlined in this book. If the role is dispersed depending upon the situation, the administrator who is leading the curriculum should fall into the leadership patterns and behaviors described in this book. The key to effective curriculum leadership is not found within job descriptions. It is found in the behavior of the leader.

For principals or other line administrators to be thrust into the role of curriculum leader is sometimes difficult. Effective principals must be skilled in individual decision-making patterns that are dictated by circumstances requiring immediate and decisive action. The same could be said for superintendents or any other district level administrative position. Such circumstances are not usually present in curriculum decision making. Also, curriculum leadership involves leading in an area where the followers are often more knowledgeable of the content than the leader. For these reasons the curriculum leader needs a new set of operating principles. This book develops this perspective.

Although servant leadership theory is being advocated, this does not mean that the circumstances dictating curriculum are always ambiguous. There are times when the curriculum leader must be decisive. The most obvious is when the curriculum leader is presenting data and evidence that accurately portray the current status of the curriculum program. A second circumstance that calls for decisive leadership is when teachers or administrators or other stakeholders advocate curriculum positions or decisions that are contrary to the data and information. Curriculum assessment needs to examine benchmarks as a means of determining the current performance. The curriculum leader must be decisive and forceful to ensure that the curriculum program is focused on the pursuit of what ought to be, not in maintaining the status quo (what is).

Servant leadership is advocated for curriculum leadership because the assumptions and principles upon which it is based are congruent with the nature of the curriculum functions in schools and the nature of the people (the teachers) who must implement the curriculum functions.

Curriculum leadership is more about process than content. Most school system's curriculum includes fourteen distinct subject areas, regardless of how the subjects are organized. Whether the curriculum is subject-based, inter disciplinary, or integrated, content will be derived from the fourteen different subject areas.

Most educators, including curriculum leaders, have from one to three subject majors. Therefore, in the role of curriculum leader, there are curriculum developments that do not coincide with the subject expertise of the curriculum leader. The subject matter expertise will come from the participants, who are drawn from the teachers within the subject matter departments. The curriculum leader is not always the subject matter specialist.

Within curriculum development beyond boilerplate standards, the process involves significant decisions, in curriculum, instruction, and assessment, for which there is not "right or wrong" answer but involves significant questions to discern upon that have many correct choices.

Needless to say, in most instances, the group being led by the servitor leader has more knowledge and/or experience in the curriculum in question than the leader. Therefore, following servitor leadership principles, the leader concentrates on how to facilitate the process in such a manner that will optimize the expertise of the group.

Critics of servant leadership often base their criticism on the assumption that servitor leaders let employees (teachers) do what they want, and thus create anarchy.

Servitor leaders do not identify and meet the wants of their people. What servitor leaders do is identify and meet the needs of their people, and serve them. Slaves do what others want, servants do what others need. There is a world of difference between meeting wants and meeting needs.[1]

A CONVERSATION ABOUT CURRICULUM LEADERSHIP

This section presents a conversation between an experienced curriculum leader and an aspiring one.

ASPIRING: If I disappeared for a year, could the school curriculum still function?

LEADER: Yes. This does not suggest that the quality of the curriculum would not be affected. It most certainly would be. However, the school could go on without you. That is probably not true of any of the other school administrators. Most certainly the principals will have to be present, so the school can operate on a day-to-day basis. The superintendent will have to conduct board business. The personnel director must hire people to run the schools, etc. But there is a curriculum in place. It may be more informal than formal. It may, in fact, be nonexistent as far as a congruent process that is uniform for subjects and grade levels. But the teachers, who are the "curriculum leaders" for their classrooms, are teaching something, so there is an operational curriculum.

The job descriptions of all the other school administrators will contain responsibilities that, if not fulfilled, would result in serious problems with the day-to-day operation of the school. For the curriculum leader, no such immediacy exists. So, the curriculum leader must work from the perspective of influence, not power or authority. The job description is somewhat frivolous. The work flow is vital.

ASPIRING: You mean to tell me that I am accountable for the quality of the curriculum program, but I don't evaluate anybody who implements the program?

LEADER: The answer is probably yes. In some instances, the curriculum leader is an assistant-superintendent-level person. Therefore, they would have authority over the principals. In other instances, the curriculum leader is parallel to the principals on the organizational chart. In other instances, the curriculum leader is under the auspices of the principal. Regardless of the organizational structure, the curriculum leader will probably not be evaluating the teachers, who are the persons implementing the curriculum.

ASPIRING: What do you mean, establish your own influence?

LEADER: Just what it says. Organizational influence comes from two sources. It's either based on position through job description or on competency or expertise through the willful assent of the client. The job description of the curriculum leader centers around processes, not decisions. The success of those processes depends upon the cooperation of others. Only through influence possessed because of competency and skill will this occur.

ASPIRING: Wait a minute. A principal is a principal; a superintendent is a superintendent is a superintendent. What position constitutes the "curriculum leader"?

LEADER: No single position. The responsibility is dispersed. That's what makes this whole issue of curriculum leadership seem ambiguous.

ASPIRING: So, when we talk about curriculum leadership we could be talking about anybody in the school organization?

LEADER: That is correct.

ASPIRING: So, I've got to be smarter than everybody else (in curriculum), but I can't flaunt it?

LEADER: Yes and yes. The position of curriculum leader is based on expertise and competency, not position. But remember, the expertise and competency is not content based. The teachers have similar or better knowledge in curriculum content. What you need are facilitation skills and communication expertise.

ASPIRING: Am I going to be a graduate student forever?

LEADER: Yes, whether or not you ever attend a university again. The school personnel look to you as the educational specialist. It may not be fair, but the general feeling is that, since you don't have a building to run or a large staff to evaluate, you must have time to be reflective and "keep up" with trends and issues. If you don't want to be a lifelong learner, you don't want to be a curriculum leader.

ASPIRING: But I'm a people person. I don't like data and statistics, and I don't know a lot about them. I'm not a bean counter.

LEADER: Better learn. Schools are accountable for student achievement. That achievement is based on testing. The tests are based on the curriculum. You can't be accountable to the public or the political structure without the proper analysis and interpretation of data. You've got to know how to present and explain the success and failures of the educational program.

ASPIRING: Since I don't seem to have too much authority can I ever be assertive in this job?

LEADER: Yes. You've got to role model the message that curriculum is important. And, you've got to show everybody why. But since you aren't in charge of anybody, but are in charge of things of importance (curriculum issues), you don't point fingers, or assign blame. You must be strong on discussing issues without having personalities or roles interfere.

ASPIRING: I hate that the students don't know who I am.

LEADER: You gave that up when you moved into the central office. The only administrators that the students know are the building-level administrators who are with them every day. If being with students and interacting with them in an ongoing manner is the most important thing to you as an educator, let's talk about how we can get you a position back in the building. How does assistant principal sound?

ASPIRING: Do the principals think I am a spy?

LEADER: That's up to you. What relationships have you built? How do you spend your days? When you go to a building, what do you do? How much efficacy do you convey in conversation with the building principals? When you are proactive, are you sensitive to legitimate obstacles and constraints that negate your position? When requested, are you reactive to their needs and expectations?

ASPIRING: Where do I go when the buildings have Christmas parties?

LEADER: Back to your office, unless you are invited. This is another perk you give up when you leave the buildings.

ASPIRING: I've heard ex-coaches make lousy curriculum leaders. Why is that?

LEADER: I'm not sure that stereotype is accurate. The statement does point out a basic difference between coaching and curriculum work. In coaching, you prepare a team for a game every week. Then, you either win or lose. Either way, it's immediate feedback and evaluation. You quickly correct mistakes and move on to the next week to see if your changes work. But curriculum is more of a long-term process. For example, a K–12 curriculum project may take one or two years to complete. The feedback is not immediate. Sometimes it takes years to see the fruits of your labor and evaluate its level of success.

You can't have a coach's mentality in curriculum work. Coaching is like a rollercoaster, up one week and down the next. Curriculum work is like a turtle traveling cross-country, a slow and long process. If you need constant and quick feedback to function effectively, curriculum leadership will probably leave you frustrated. But if you buy into the continuous improvement concept, curriculum work is pretty satisfying.

THE UNIQUE NATURE OF CURRICULUM LEADERSHIP

The aims of the curriculum program for any school system are the same as for the other organizational functions; namely, quality, accountability, effectiveness, efficiency, continuous improvement, high morale, and extensive involvement. So the question naturally arises as to why and how curriculum leadership is unique. Why not just read a book or watch a DVD or video on administrative leadership? So let's examine the ways that curriculum leadership is different and unique from other educational leadership functions.

- *Curriculum leadership is defined more by the concept than the organizational position.*

  - The job description or work flowchart for most administrative positions clearly indicates areas of responsibility. Superintendents, principals, business managers, personnel directors, and supervisors have clearly delineated tasks and decisions for which they are held accountable. They may decide to delegate, but the leadership is clearly defined as being a part of their position. In addition, the persons occupying those positions have within their capacity the control of the organizational variables necessary to effectively administer their role. Such factors are not necessarily present for the curriculum leadership position. The school is pledged to have an effective curriculum program, but that is possible only if many people other than the curriculum leader are committed to seeing it done. Therefore, the curriculum leader lacks the authority to force processes and products to conclusion through chain-of-command power. Instead, they must build relationships that will motivate other key educators in the organization, notably the principals and teachers, to implement the curriculum program mission, vision, and goals.

- *Curriculum leader competency is in process, not content.*

  - In school systems, teachers will not claim to have the level of expertise that is necessary to be a principal or superintendent. The tasks performed and the decisions made at these organizational levels are not part of a teacher's professional training. Administrative functions such as scheduling, budgeting, public relations, law, and policy are taught only in graduate programs designed to train educational administrators. However, all teachers claim expertise in their subject area. The curriculum leader is asked to lead curriculum development in as many as fourteen different content fields. Except when they are leading a curriculum development in their own teaching field, the expertise level of the people they are leading—the teachers—is greater in content knowledge than that of the curriculum leader. Therefore, the nature of the decision-making process is different. The curriculum leader is the expert in facilitation, but the teachers are the experts in content. The vital competency for the curriculum leader is facilitation skills that will create the environment in which the teachers will make wise content decisions.

- *The curriculum leader lacks the direct link to the operations level.*

  - Teachers are under the direct supervision of the principal. Included in the responsibilities of principals and assistant principals is the supervision of instruction. Therefore, they are the administrators who observe the planned curriculum in operation. Thus they are seeing the "actual" curriculum on a day-to-day basis. The curriculum leader is not performing this function. Therefore, they must rely on the relationship with the building principal to gain access to teachers concerning any facet of the implementation phase of the planned curriculum.

- *The curriculum leader can never use immediacy as a rationale for administrative action.*

  - If the principal of the building said, "I'm not going to make out a schedule. You teachers do whatever you want," the school would be thrown into chaos. If the superintendent failed to allocate the budget by categories, the treasurer could not pay bills or endorse purchase orders, so the school could not continue to operate. If the maintenance people didn't see to it that there is heat and electricity in the buildings, the school would have to close.
  - However, if the curriculum leader said, "We have no planned curriculum, you teachers teach whatever you wish," the school could continue to operate indefinitely. In this case, the curriculum might lack continuity and articulation, but classes would go on. Why? Because even if formal curriculum development does not occur, the school's educational program will operate anyway, since this is the only aspect of school operation and management that teachers are trained to perform alone. Namely, they develop and deliver the curriculum.

- *Curriculum leadership* is *nonauthoritarian in nature.*

  - Curriculum leadership calls for the use of many different styles. Sometimes it demands servitor, or mentor, or advocate, or facilitator, or instructor. But it almost always demands nonauthoritarian behavior, except when presenting hard data that is irrefutable and vital to the curriculum assessment process. Nonauthoritarian leadership is called for because curriculum leadership has one purpose: to ensure involvement and responsiveness/ownership by the principals and teachers in the curriculum design and implementation. All staff should have a sense of ownership over the process.

- *For the curriculum leader, task and relationships are inseparable.*

  - Administrative theory divides the role function by task and relationships. Specific theories such as Blake's Power Cycle indicate that, depending on the situation, either a task or a relationship demeanor is called for. The assumption is that sometimes an administrator is called upon to perform or dictate to others tasks that need to be accomplished for the effective operation of the school. It's something that has to be done, so somebody is told to do it. Now! Relationship building is either not called for, or there isn't time to pursue. For the line administrator, this is clear delineation. They have the authority to see that whoever is responsible for this task, through either board or administrative policy, gets it done.

- For the curriculum leader, no such clear delineation is present. The tasks involved in curriculum development are not part of anyone's job description. Therefore, the curriculum leader must rely upon relationships that are strong enough to sustain the accomplishment of the tasks.

- *The curriculum leader must have a strong ego and confidence in their importance to the success of the school curriculum.*

  - There is an old, worn-out administration joke that goes like this: Question— How many R's in curriculum? Answer—Who cares? This joke symbol- izes the attitude of school administrators who do not regard curriculum as a high priority. This attitude leads them to place all facets of curricu- lum, from development to assessment, in a low priority. In school sys- tems where a significant number of the administrators have this attitude, apathy toward curriculum becomes an organizational climate. Curricu- lum leaders must not let this prevailing attitude defeat them. They must have confidence that once the teachers, community, and administrators see the contribution that effective curriculum processes make to school accountability, the anticurriculum climate will cease.

- *The curriculum leader must learn two languages: the language of educa- tion and the language of the public.*

  - How many times have you heard an educator say, "We'll never get the public to understand this?" Or "This is too complicated for the layman to comprehend," or "If we tell the public this, they will misinterpret the information." These are unacceptable responses to educational account- ability. Somebody in the school system must know how to explain to all the different audiences and stakeholders in education the meaning of the educational program and its results. The curriculum leader is a person equipped to do this. A weakness of some curriculum leaders is that they can communicate with only one of the audiences, that is, either the educational audiences or the public audiences. For a school system to be effective, all stakeholders must interact with the school on the educational program. This is not a public relations strategy; it is a communication strategy. It is not an attempt to convince the public or the teachers that the school system is a good one. It is an attempt to explain in fair terms the status of the educational program, and its successes and failures in a manner all involved can understand.

- You do not have to be weak, nonassertive, or reactive to be an effective curriculum leader. But neither can you be a Neanderthal. You must have the knowledge and the communication skills to explain all aspects of curriculum to audiences of different levels of sophistication.

- *The curriculum leader must be knowledgeable and skilled in data analysis.*

  - Did you think that when you finished graduate school you would never use statistics again? And did you think that research was an abstract concept for doctoral students? Well, guess what? The curriculum leader needs to use both of these orientations to be effective. The assessment of curriculum will be based on both qualitative and quantitative methods. Gone are the days when schools evaluated themselves based on informal feedback. Data must be used in all assessment. The curriculum leader is the person looked to for the analysis, synthesis, and evaluation of the data that describes the educational program. This includes the effective use of technology and data analytics. There are many data sets available, how these sets are utilized will set apart the successful curriculum direction from non effective processes.

- *The curriculum leader must be reflective.*

  - Here is a story for you. Once upon a time, a parent came to the superintendent's office to complain about an administrator whom he said spent too much of each day looking out his office window. The parent knew this because he lived across the street from the school offices. The parent asked the superintendent, "What is his job, anyway?" The superintendent replied, "He is in charge of curriculum and staff development." The parent asked, "And what are the results of his work?" The superintendent replied, "Because of his leadership, we have high morale and involvement in curriculum in the teaching staff, 100 percent implementation of the planned curriculum, 100 percent match between our planned curriculum and the state and local testing programs, and we rank in the highest category in every educational standard the state uses to evaluate schools." The parent replied, "Make sure you have enough money in your budget for glass cleaner. *I* want his window cleaned daily."
  - The nature of day-to-day work in schools makes it hard for principals and teachers to be reflective. The natural work function of teachers calls for a fast-paced schedule, complete with a thirty-minute lunch. Students are demanding of their teachers' time for everything from tutoring to

discipline. Planning time is often taken up with grading papers, requiring other times for planning the next day's lesson.

Principals spend many days going through a myriad of short, unrelated tasks that are physically and emotionally draining. If there is a lull in the day, the principal is grateful for the break but lacks the psychological or emotional resources to use the time for philosophical reflection.

However, the curriculum leader does not have a building to operate nor a large number of people to supervise. To reiterate, curriculum leadership is conceptual, not positional. Barker (1995) says that paradigm shifts come from the outside, or on the fringes. The curriculum leader is on the fringes of the day-to-day operation of the school. He has time to think, to ponder, to dream, to view the school from the perspective of what ought to be, not what is. This reflection can produce innovation, elimination of deficiencies, and continuous improvement. The curriculum leader should be the paradigm pioneer for the school and lead the administrative team in asking the paradigm-shifting question: What is it today that is impossible to do, but if we could, would fundamentally change the way we educate people?

LEADING THE HIDDEN (COLLATERAL) CURRICULUM

The term *hidden curriculum* refers to unofficial instructional influences, which may or may not support the planned curriculum. Hidden curriculum infers that some of the outcomes of schooling are not covered in the formal or planned curriculum. Therefore, they are not formally recognized as a part of the curriculum. The hidden curriculum can be a powerful detriment to the planned curriculum or a powerful advocate for it. The concept of hidden curriculum gives rise to several questions: From whom is it hidden? Students? Teachers? Administrators? Of course, the most important question for the curriculum leader is, what do we do with it when we find it? Should we leave it unstudied, hidden, and treat it as a natural aspect of the school experience? Before we answer this question, let's delve deeper into what is meant by the hidden curriculum.

C. Wayne Gordon was one of the first to reveal an informal system that affected what was learned—the hidden curriculum. In his book *The Social System of the High School,* Gordon advanced the theory that the behavior of high school students is related to their role and status in the school. Furthermore, these roles and status are a subsystem of the community and the larger context of U.S. society.[2]

In addition to the formal curriculum, which is defined by the written curriculum and learning materials, students are also subject to an informal system defined by clubs, activities, and unrecognized cliques, factions, and other groups. This informal system creates a network of personal and social relationships that have tremendous influence on the learning of each student.

The hidden curriculum is not all that hidden. It is very powerful. Therefore, the curriculum leader should be aware of its existence and try to empower its positive aspects and counter its negative aspects. The hidden curriculum is best studied by watching the strategies the students use to cope with the school's regimen. Their reactions create atmospheres that may produce conformists, rebels, recluses, cheats, or other socialization results.

The hidden curriculum may consist of functions that are neither intended nor recognized. Sometimes courses and other planned experiences benefit some special interest group more than the students. The most negative hidden curriculum is the subtle, discriminating way that the school's environment or atmosphere discredits the dreams, experiences, and knowledge of students from specific gender, class, and racial groups.

The hidden curriculum can be a vehicle for moral growth. It can reflect an atmosphere of justice, giving equal worth to all types of students. This curriculum, more than the formal curriculum, determines to a significant degree the participants' sense of self-worth and self-esteem. The hidden curriculum is a determining factor in the integration of students, interactions across race and status, friendships, communications, and cultural understanding.

Suggestions for making the hidden curriculum more consistent with the aims of the formal curriculum have been proposed as a means of ensuring that the hidden curriculum is a positive one. Henry Giroux recommends such actions as doing away with those properties of the hidden curriculum that are associated with alienation: rigid time schedules, tracking, testing, content fragmentation, and competition.[3]

Catherine Cornbleth notes that formal curriculum fosters conformity to national ideals and social conventions, whereas the hidden curriculum maintains social, economic, and cultural inequalities.[4] To make the hidden curriculum consistent with formal curriculum, school leaders must examine the consequences of specific conditions in the school with regard to three categories:

1. Organizational functions such as time, facilities, and materials
2. Interpersonal relations, including student-teacher, teacher-administrator, teacher-parent, and student-students
3. Institutional policies, routine procedures, rituals, social structures, and extracurricular activities available to the students

Curriculum leaders should find out if these structures and practices are consistent with the mission and vision of the school and promote the human potential and social justice for all students.

The continual reliance on educational accountability based on student test scores have created an excessive concern for specificity in setting learning objectives and assessment through standardized achievement tests. These norm-referenced tests, plus many teacher-made assessments, focus on recall and narrow skills, thus placing undue emphasis on the lower cognitive levels. This results in schooling being a production process as opposed to a growth process. Moreover, these practices are based on the questionable assumption that students learn only the particular things that the planned curriculum has targeted for them. Yet unanticipated collateral learning from the hidden curriculum may be far more significant to the pupil than targeted curriculum.

Dewey noted that much of the knowledge and technical material contained in the planned curriculum is eventually forgotten and has to be learned over again in a different form, or it actually has to be unlearned, if the student is to make progress intellectually. But collateral learning, resulting from the hidden curriculum, may create enduring attitudes toward what is learned and toward learning itself, and may count more in a student's future because such learning governs whether or not they will have the desire to continue growing intellectually.

Acknowledgment of the hidden curriculum, and the collateral learning that it produces, means that the learning is not accidental learning. It derives from a planned curriculum that engages the student in emergent learning situations, ensuring that the curriculum is not limited to established convergent experiences. In fact, the hidden curriculum cannot really be hidden when human variability rather than predictability is valued.

THE NULL CURRICULUM

The null curriculum is more important now than ever, due to the knowledge explosion. This knowledge explosion has created the need for schools to engage in curriculum abandonment. Thus the percentage of knowledge that students are exposed to through the planned curriculum grows smaller each school year. The danger of this abandonment process is that it will create more convergent thinking, thus negating the effect of the hidden curriculum. If the curriculum abandonment process is not accompanied by an emphasis on research and lifelong learning skills and attitudes, then the school is conveying that they have taught everything worth teaching. Therefore, the null curriculum should be approached from three perspectives:

1. The prioritizing of knowledge and skills for all curriculum areas must be reached through consensus of the stakeholders.

2. The research skills must be taught with the intent of allowing all students to become lifelong learners, and at the appropriate time, pursue the null curriculum.
3. The school, through the hidden curriculum, must demonstrate to the student that learning is an individual emancipation to be pursued as the spirit and imagination of each person leads them.

Leadership for the hidden curriculum is going to have to be a team effort. If the school has a curriculum leadership position from the central office, that person will lead the development of the planned curriculum. The hidden curriculum, however, will be influenced by the building administrators, teachers, classified personnel, parents, community attitudes, and any other adults and students who are present in the school environment each day.

Therefore, attention to the hidden curriculum must be an ongoing process that identifies the roles of all informal groups, the motivations within the groups, and the place of individuals within the groups. In addition, school personnel must continually examine what cognitive and affective procedures and policies are either promoting the dreams, aspirations, and knowledge of students or subtly discriminating against them due to specific gender, race, ethnic background, or ability, and take appropriate action to encourage the positive hidden curriculum and reduce the effect of the negative hidden curriculum.

CONCLUSION

Throughout the remainder of this book, all aspects of the curriculum program will be presented and discussed. The effective use of the leadership principles presented in this chapter should be followed in all the processes, tasks, and decision making; this servitor leadership style, combined with a data-based approach, provides the best opportunity to achieve not only the ultimate aim of curriculum leadership, responsiveness, involvement, commitment, and ownership of the planned curriculum but also the presence of a positive hidden curriculum that supports and augments the planned curriculum.

NOTES

1. James C. Hunter, *The Servant* (Roseville, CA: Prima Publishing, 1998), 65.
2. C. Wayne Gordon, *The Social System of the High School* (Glencoe, IL: Free Press, 1957).

3. Henry A. Giroux, "Developing Educational Programs: Overcoming the Hidden Curriculum." *The Clearing House* 52, no. 4 (December 1978): 148–152.

4. Catherine Cornbleth, "Beyond Hidden Curriculum." *Journal of Curriculum Studies* 16, no. 16 (1984): 29–36.

REFERENCES

Barker, Joel A. (1995). *The business of paradigms* (videotape). Burnsville, MN: Clearhouse Learning Corporation.

Dewey, John. (1938). *Experience in education*, 48. New York: Macmillan.

Hensen, Kenneth T. (2001). *Curriculum planning: Integrating multiculturalism, c, and education reform*. Boston: McGraw-Hill

Jenkins, Lee. (1997). *Improving student learning: Applying deming's quality principles in classrooms*. Milwaukee, WI: ASQ Quality Press.

McCutcheon, Gail. (1995). *Developing the curriculum: Solo and group deliberation*. White Plains, NY: Longman.

McNeil, John. (1996). *Curriculum: A c introduction*, 5th ed. New York: HarperCollins.

Reinhartz, Judy, and Don M. Beach. (1992). *Secondary education: Focus on curriculum*. New York: HarperCollins.

Tanner, Daniel, and Laurel Tanner. (1995). *Curriculum development: Theory into practice*, 3rd ed. Englewood Cliffs, NJ: Merrill/Prentice-Hall.

Chapter 3

Principles and Operational Definitions of Curriculum

THE PURPOSE OF CURRICULUM

The essential purpose of curriculum is to provide guidance for the educators who work in schools. This work strives to provide practical strategies and solutions for the "how to" of curriculum work. The work is pragmatic in nature and deals with concrete concepts in curriculum, such as the following:

• Design
• Development
• Implementation
• Evaluation

This approach to the study of curriculum is based on the rationale first proposed by Ralph Tyler.[1] The Tyler rationale states that curriculum work should address four issues:

1. What educational purpose should the school seek to attain?
2. What educational experiences can be provided that are likely to attain these purposes?
3. How can these educational experiences be effectively organized?
4. How can we determine whether or not these purposes are being attained?

Tyler's rationale, which is over seventy years old, is a linear model. It suggests that the four steps occur in a sequential manner. It is useful to place Tyler's questions in a cyclical model to reflect modern strategic planning and continuous improvement principles.

By rephrasing the original four questions and adding a fifth, curriculum workers can apply Tyler's principles to the contemporary school. This rephrasing can also reflect the role of the various stakeholders, both educational and political, who are influencing curriculum decision making today. These five questions are:

- What educational purposes is this school, district, or state seeking to attain? Note: Based on the current national debate about education, and not withstanding that education is primarily a state function, one could argue that the federal government is also attempting to seek and attain specific educational purposes.
- Are we providing a range of learning experiences that are likely to facilitate the attainment of our school's educational purpose?
- Are we effectively organizing those learning experiences and making them readily available to students?
- How well are we determining that the school's educational purposes are being attained (by means of those learning experiences we have provided, organized, and made available to students)?
- Are we striving to maintain dynamic interrelatedness (i.e., wholeness) and systemic thinking among curricular activities called for by the first four questions by continuously reasking and reanswering these questions?

The last point, proposed by Komoski,[2] is a Total Quality concept that is used in modern organizations in the quest for continuous improvement. It is best illustrated through the use of the Plan-Do-Study-Act (PDSA) cycle pictured in figures 3.1 and 3.2. The first four questions would be asked in the Plan cycle of defining the system, assessing the current situation, and analyzing causes. The Do-Study-Act cycle would implement the improvement theory (curriculum design and implementation), and then the cycle would continuously repeat itself.

Through the use of PDSA cycle, the curriculum process would become a continuous process that would eliminate curriculum development time lines that relegate the study and revision of curriculum to periodic reviews. The principles that Tyler gave us in 1950 are still the relevant questions concerning curriculum design. However, the methods used to pursue his rationale are based in continuous quality improvement, and they are closer to the works of Deming, Scholtes, and other Total Quality authors.

There are differing views on the purpose of curriculum. These views seem to fall into three categories: organizational control, stakeholder consensus, and individual emancipation, as described in the following sections.

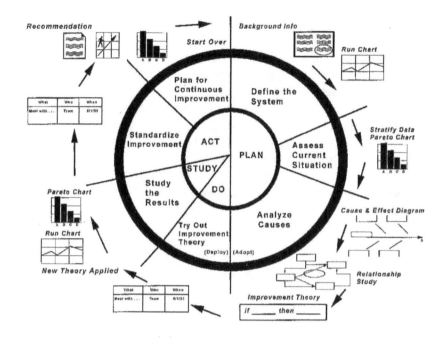

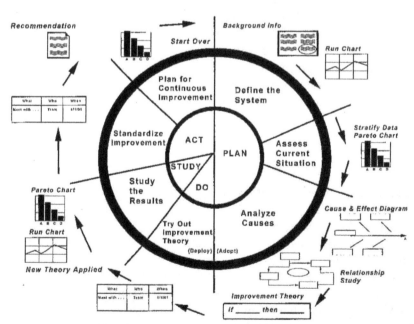

Figures 3.1 and 3.2.   Plan-Do-Study-Act (PDSA) Cycle. Adopted from Koalty Kid Pocket Tools, PQ Systems by Stan Laferty, Clermont County Educational Service Center, Batavia, Ohio

Organizational Control

Organizational control refers to defining the elements or variables involved in curriculum and developing and implementing a system of decision making for curriculum design.

This view suggests that there is a "right" curriculum. It is a political viewpoint that the schools should be teaching certain things and that a system of control is needed to ensure that the schools do what they are supposed to do. State legislatures promote this view by mandating specific courses and/or proficiency tests. The assumption is that control of what is taught in the schools is the purpose of curriculum. Boards of education or administrations that mandate and supervise close adherence to curriculum designs demonstrate an orientation to this view.

To be ethical, this viewpoint must be based on reliable data or information. For example, a school system may mandate learning objectives based on the fact that standardized testing results show that the students are not achieving to their potential. To mandate learning objectives that have no basis in data would be imposing orthodoxy and contracting the spectrum of knowledge without a legitimate reason.

This purpose of curriculum should concentrate on basic skills and exercise the level of control necessary to ensure that all students are receiving proper instruction in the "boilerplate" domain of the curriculum.

This purpose currently dominates public school curriculum. From the federal level, common core, accountability models based on paper-and-pencil testing, the priority given to the charter schools based on mandated standards different from those imposed on public schools, block grants based on tighter controls over curriculum, and funding that promotes these initiatives have an organizational control purpose.

Stakeholder Consensus

Stakeholder consensus is defined as a practical interest in what goes on in the classroom. It is grounded in the assumption that conflicts can be resolved through mutual social expectations.

This view promotes the belief that all the stakeholders within the educational community should work toward consensus as to what the schools should teach. This is the view that is most commonly used in school systems. It is a very practical approach that gives much credence to "best practice." The view is like the control view in that it still approaches curriculum decision making from an organizational perspective, that is, a curriculum exists that can satisfy the needs of all the students. It is also imperative in consensus that the curriculum should be mutually agreed to by all the school's stakeholders.

Needless to say, consensus would be pursued with the full knowledge and utilization of data and information concerning the level of success of the students on the current curriculum. Since a universally accepted principle of curriculum implementation is that teacher involvement in curriculum equals teacher commitment to curriculum, the consensus purpose of curriculum is very significant to the curriculum leader. It is in this area that the curriculum leader can exert the most influence. Therefore, it is the curriculum purpose that requires the most effective leadership behavior. In an effective school that is focused on student needs and achievement, the consensus purpose will utilize more resources than control and emancipation.

Individual Emancipation

Individual emancipation is concerned with person-centered curriculums that liberate individuals through dialogic self-reflection. This view of curriculum is one based on individual needs and expectations. Proponents of this view would deny the common curriculum for all students that is practiced in most schools. This is an intellectual view that rejects organizational control and decision making. Instead, curriculum should be based on the needs of each individual. The view seems to suggest that conformity has no place in education, that diversity is the strength and purpose of curriculum. Said another way, curriculum serves the individual's self-reflection. In no way should curriculum restrict or contain the learning opportunities of the individual. Needless to say, this view is not based on practicality in relation to the current emphasis on accountability for K–12 curriculum. It is difficult to see how it could even function in the current public school setting unless you view it as a philosophy used in conjunction with control and consensus. However, for elective curriculum in the elementary and secondary schools and for the upper echelons of formal education, such as undergraduate and graduate school, the emancipation view is easier to conceptualize.

In the current political climate, which seems determined to use standardized student testing as the major, if not the sole criterion for school accountability, emancipation is not receiving much attention in curriculum theory and practice. But for any school interested in meeting the curriculum needs of all its students, even the ones on the fringe, regardless of the cost, emancipation as a curriculum purpose is a necessity. This purpose recognizes that for some students control and consensus are not sufficient.

Needless to say, all schools are trying to create individuals who will be reflective and lifelong learners. Such goals will be pursued in curriculum design as well as implementation. In the context of this discussion, emancipation is defined as a unique and separate purpose.

CURRICULUM LEADERSHIP TO ACHIEVE ORGANIZATIONAL CONTROL, STAKEHOLDER CONSENSUS, AND INDIVIDUAL EMANCIPATION FOR STUDENTS

Organizational Control

Curriculum control leadership is exercised within the boilerplate content areas. This is the basic skill part of the curriculum. The content is universal for all students. This part of curriculum is the basis for universal testing of students. The tests may be required either locally or by the state. The boilerplate curriculum contains the proficiencies and competencies that are required for promotion or graduation. There is no decision about whether or not to include the boilerplate content in the planned curriculum; it has to be there. The curriculum leadership question is how to best ensure that there is congruence among the written (planned) curriculum, instruction, and the testing program. This analysis requires intensive study of the scope, which means the learning objectives, and sequence, which is the order in which the objectives are taught, to ensure complete and timely teaching of the basic skills based on the testing program.

The biggest challenge to the curriculum leader is how to create ownership of and responsiveness from the teachers regarding this aspect of the curriculum. The control curriculum violates all the principles of effective curriculum design. First, it is developed without local teacher input. Second, it begins with assessment, which means it creates a learning environment based on teaching to the test. Since control has the most political clout, it takes precedence over the other purposes. The curriculum leader must strive to create a positive attitude among teachers and administrators toward the control purpose of curriculum. They must stress the fact that once a school is accountable for this aspect of the program, more attention and focus can be given to the other curriculum purposes.

Like it or not, schools are a part of the larger political spectrum and, therefore, susceptible to the political winds of the times. The curriculum leader should take the position that a large portion of the boilerplate curriculum would have been included in the planned curriculum if local consensus had been part of the process. As a curriculum leader, you must take ownership and stress this fact. Do not use the state mandates as a cop-out. Do not approach the control purpose as something you wouldn't do if the state was not making you do it. This attitude will rub off on the teachers. Every school has a basic core curriculum for which all students are held accountable. Be positive. Remember the old adage, "God grant me the serenity to accept the things I cannot change, change the things I can, and the wisdom to know the difference." Being the curriculum leader in control curriculum is like being the relief pitcher who inherits a bases-loaded situation. He didn't put the runners on, but he's got to do his best to see that they don't score. Likewise, the curriculum leader didn't establish the boilerplate, but he must see to it that the students and teachers achieve its aim.

Stakeholder Consensus

Effective school curriculum programs have a common goal—the involvement, responsiveness, commitment, and thus ownership of the curriculum design and implementation by all stakeholders. It's the curriculum leader's role to see that this goal is met. The key is process expertise in facilitation and communication. This curriculum purpose requires decision making regarding the curriculum content. That is the role of the content specialists. The curriculum leader's role is to facilitate a process that will ensure the implementation of the planned curriculum by teachers who want to respond and own the content of the curriculum.

Consensus is needed in the locally developed required curriculum as well as the elective curriculum. Both of these curriculums go beyond basic skills and will vary from school to school, based on the needs of each school's students.

However, the important issue here is not content. Research and best practice have long indicated that too many school systems do not implement the planned curriculum to the extent necessary to achieve accountability for vertical and horizontal articulation. Why else would the literature be full of such terms as the following:

- Recommended curriculum
- Written curriculum
- Supported curriculum
- Taught curriculum
- Tested curriculum
- Learned curriculum
- Hidden curriculum

These multiple definitions indicate that various degrees of commitment and ownership of the school curriculum exist. In the consensus purpose, it is the curriculum leader's role to serve as a guide in the creation of one operational definition of curriculum.

Individual Emancipation

Although the law has never required that schools maximize the potential of every student who is deemed nonliable, every student body has people for whom the control and consensus purposes of curriculum fall short. Highly motivated students, gifted students, and students with high interest in one particular area need the school to accommodate these highly individualistic needs. Perhaps curriculum emancipation occurs as much in differentiated instruction as in planned differentiated curriculum. However, to achieve the emancipation purpose of curriculum, curriculum planning and documents must promote inquiry, lifelong learning goals, and the joy of learning— acquiring knowledge for its own sake. The curriculum leader should begin curriculum development by establishing how the development fits the vision and mission of the school. If that vision includes inquiry, lifelong learning, and the desire to leave no child behind, emancipation is a curriculum purpose to be pursued.

In a world dominated by accountability and learning objectives, emancipation as a curriculum purpose is sometimes overlooked. The curriculum leader must keep the concept present in the minds and hearts of the content decision makers. The Mozarts, Picassos, and Einsteins of the future are in our schools. We must let them breathe and flourish. Our world demands it.

KEY OPERATIONAL DEFINITIONS

One factor that has caused problems in curriculum development is the lack of universally accepted definitions. The solution to this problem is for the school to utilize operational definitions.

An operational definition makes no claim to universal truth or acceptance. It simply states that for this school system, the definition has a specific meaning. By using operational definitions, the school organization can spend its time and resources on implementing the operational definitions rather than wasting valuable time on rhetorical discussions about what the definitions mean.

In curriculum design, development, and evaluation, five terms particularly need to be clarified so that dialogue can be productive and efficient. These terms are *curriculum, instruction, teaching, vertical articulation*, and *horizontal articulation*.

- Curriculum: The curriculum is the plan made for guiding learning in the schools, usually represented in retrievable documents (or technology) of several levels of generality, and the actualization of those plans in the classroom, as experienced by the learner and as recorded by an observer (usually the teacher). Those experiences take place in a learning environment that also influences what is learned.[3]
- Instruction: Instruction is the implementation phase of curriculum. It refers to the learning activities, inside the classroom and out, that are specifically designed to meet the goals or outcomes of the planned curriculum.

- Teaching: Teaching refers to those activities that occur in learning settings that are not a part of the planned curriculum. Events, human relationships, and other unplanned learning experiences are bound to occur during the school day. When these unplanned learning experiences take place, teaching is occurring, but not instruction. However, these "teachable moments" are a valuable part of schooling and, despite the needed emphasis on student accountability, should not be discouraged.

These two operational definitions, *instruction* and *teaching*, are offered as a means of legitimizing the two types of curriculum that occur daily in classrooms and to clarify their differences and aims.

- Vertical articulation: The term *articulation* refers to the vertical communication among teachers at various levels of schooling (primary, intermediate, middle, secondary, etc.). Articulation issues include prerequisites, scope and sequence, assessment, and abandonment. How are formal and informal communication structures established and maintained?
- Horizontal articulation: Because most modern schools are organized in such a way that more than one teacher is responsible for the same grade level (or its equivalent) or subject, horizontal communication is required to assure the desired commonality of learning experiences. This dialogue among teachers of the same grade level or subject, or multiple sections of the same course, is referred to as horizontal articulation.

NOTES

1. R. W. Tyler, *Basic Principles of Curriculum and Instruction* (Chicago: University of Chicago Press, 1950), 10.

2. P. K. Komoski, "Needed: A Whole Curriculum Approach." *Educational Leadership* 47 (February 1990): 72–77.

3. Allan A. Glatthorn, *Curriculum Leadership* (Glenview, IL: Scott Foresman, 1987), 3.

Chapter 4

Curriculum Development Process

Through the curriculum development process, a curriculum guide, or course of study, is developed to direct teachers in their teaching. The guide is a structured plan, which can range from very specific to a broad outline. It is often organized as grade specific or content specific and includes standards, objectives, or other performance measures that students are expected to meet.

These standards, also known as student learning standards or academic standards, specify what students should know and be able to do in grades K–12 and have existed since the early 1900s. Generally, standards were developed and adopted by each school, district, county, and/or state and were included in curriculum guides. Historical events have played a major role in defining standards and specifying who was responsible for developing them.

The Elementary Secondary Education Act (ESEA, 1965) has been acknowledged as the most far-reaching federal law impacting education. In an effort to close the achievement gap, especially among students from low-income families, the act underscored equal access to education and established high standards and accountability. The act "despite provisions against a national curriculum, set standards for achievement."[1]

In 1983 the Commission on Excellence published a bleak report, "A Nation at Risk: The Imperative for Educational Reform," that described American schools as falling when compared internationally. The Commission underscored the idea that all children, "regardless of race or class or economic status," were entitled to an equal education. The report emphasized that school curriculums, or academic standards, had become weak and were without purpose. It was recommended that schools adopt more rigorous and measureable standards.[2] The Improving America's Schools Act (IASA, 1994) reiterated the need for demanding standards. "In an increasingly complex and diverse society and an economic environment that will be dominated by high-skilled jobs, today's students must meet high academic standards in order to succeed."[3]

Likewise, other legislation was enacted in an effort to improve American school, such as Goals 2000 (1994); the reauthorization of the ESEA seven times, including the No Child Left Behind Act (NCLB, 2002), which concentrated on two subjects—English language arts and mathematics; and Race to the Top (2009), which funded programs focused on innovation and reform in K–12 education.

In 2009 governors and state educational leaders not only acknowledged the inconsistency in learning standards across states but also recognized that states had different definitions for student proficiency. This lack of standardization led forty-eight states to create the Common Core Standards to ensure all high school graduates were college and/or career ready.

The Common Core Standards drew adverse criticism, especially when the federal government included them as a means for holding schools accountable for student achievement through standardized tests and for narrowing the curriculum by focusing on a small subset of subjects. So, in 2015 with the passage of the Every Student Succeeds Act (ESSA), the responsibility of developing and adopting academic standards was placed with the states. In fact, "the U.S. Secretary of Education is expressly prohibited from forcing or even encouraging states to pick particular set of standards, including the Common Core."[4]

Graham (2013) reports, "In the 30 years since [the Nation at Risk's] scathing indictment, most schools have taken drastic steps to meet the report's challenge to adopt 'more rigorous and measurable standards' for learning. All states have adopted academic standards."[5] Meanwhile, school districts, county schools, and independent schools have shifted their focus and time from developing learning standards to aligning curriculum and providing meaningful curricular resources, such as curriculum maps, pacing guides, instructional frameworks, common assessments, and other resources for teachers. Chapter 6 describes this in more detail.

Only time will reveal the future direction of curriculum development. Will the federal government involvement return? Or will states continue to develop academic standards? Or will the movement once again swing responsibility back toward local schools, districts, and counties? No matter which way the direction shifts, schools will always be involved in some aspect of curriculum development. Be it developing learning objectives, aligning instructional lessons with the curriculum, and/or developing instructional resource guides, each school, district, county, and/or state utilizes an identical curriculum process.

CURRICULUM PROCESS

The Curriculum Process Flowchart (figure 4.1) depicts the process used by states or local educational organizations to develop, revise, or align academic standards, and also to develop, revise, or align instructional resources using

Form Curriculum Consortium

Select Workshop Participants

Develop Working Model

Preparatory Model   Dialogue Model
(Participant Preparation
for planning workshop)

Planning   Planning
Workshop   Workshop

Staff Input   Staff Input

Feedback   Feedback
Workshop   Workshop

Staff Input   Staff Input
(if necessary)   (if necessary)

Feedback   Feedback
Workshop   Workshop

The cycle of feedback workshop to staff input and back to feedback workshop will continue for as long as necessary to produce:

Consensus/Responsiveness/Ownership/Involvement/Commitment

Figure 4.1. Curriculum Process Flowchart

either the dialogue or preparatory model. All the steps for the two models are identical with the exception of participant preparation for the process.

In the preparatory model, the participants are asked to make individual preparation for the initial workshop (herein referred to as the planning workshop). In the dialogue model, no such preparation is used. In chapter 5, "Curriculum Decision Making," these two processes are discussed in detail, and the characteristics and rationale for each model are presented.

The process described in this chapter to develop, revise, or align curriculum or to develop instructional resources is designed to achieve consensus, responsiveness, ownership, involvement, and commitment among the stakeholders of the school's curriculum (students, teacher, administrators, parents, community). When these characteristics are present among the stakeholders, the chances that the planned curriculum will be the actual classroom curriculum are maximized. In addition, the process will ensure the highest-quality curriculum design and implementation in both content and format.

Forming Curriculum Consortia

A consortium is defined as a combination of schools involved in curriculum design and implementation. Consortia can range from very narrow to very broad in scope. The narrowest consortia would be more than one school building from the same district. The broadest would be an international group working together in curriculum endeavors. The most common curriculum consortia in schools are (see figure 4.2):

- Buildings with a school district (campus level)
- Multiple school districts within a governance jurisdiction, such as a group of schools being served by the same intermediate agency
- Regional alignments, such as a geographical area of a state
- All the schools of a state
- A national effort

The common thread that runs through all of these consortiums is that they are based on geography or governance (e.g., county, religious, or charter schools, or schools in a state), or a combination of both. It has been the accepted paradigm in curriculum design and delivery that these two factors should be the determiners of curriculum consortiums. It is suggested here that the current paradigm, based on an extension of the governance structure of the schools without regard to other educational considerations that affect curriculum, is a flawed paradigm. Therefore, it has not served schools well and is one of the primary reasons that curriculum has not achieved its potential

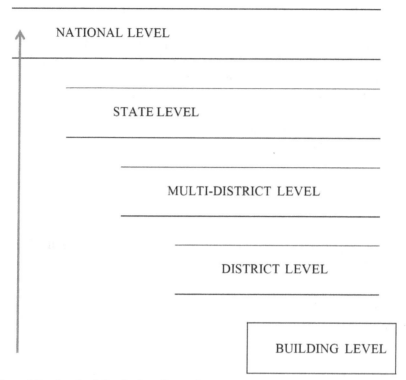

Figure 4.2. Levels of Curriculum Consortia

for positively driving student achievement The current paradigm should be abandoned in favor of curriculum consortiums based on common educational philosophy and learning materials, resources, and technology.

A NEW CURRICULUM CONSORTIUM PARADIGM

Curriculum consortiums should be based on two components: (1) commonality in educational philosophy and (2) learning materials, resources, and technology. No curriculum consortium should extend beyond the point where these two components are not common elements among all the schools participating in the consortium.

Throughout the history of curriculum consortiums, the problems have been teacher commitment or responsiveness to content decision making, and the lack of congruence between the planned curriculum and learning materials. The first problem can be solved only if the schools within the consortium have a common philosophy, thus making effective content decision making feasible. The second problem can be solved only if the schools are using common learning materials, resources, and technology. Since schools across a state have varying access to resources from abundance to disparity, and including various numbers of schools, it becomes difficult to achieve congruency. As discussed later, alternative approaches to curriculum development can minimize an incongruent curriculum consortium.

Both elements, common philosophy and congruence in relation to learning materials, resources, and technology, must be present for a successful curriculum consortium.

RESULTS OF AN OVEREXTENDED
CURRICULUM CONSORTIUM

When the curriculum consortium is overextended, one or more of the following can result.

Ambiguous Content

The most common method used to resolve conflict in consensus decision making is to move to higher levels of generalization. The danger of this method in curriculum decisions is that the generalization becomes so abstract that it is of little value in guiding the implementation of the decision. For example, if the group were trying to decide the learning standards, goals, or objectives for the topic of abortion, consensus would be difficult to obtain.

If the group keeps moving to higher levels of generalization to reach consensus, they would eventually reach the point where the discussion would center on valuing life. At that level of generalization, consensus could probably be reached. However, that decision would have no value in driving curriculum, learning standards, or instruction. To be effective, curriculum design must produce learning outcomes or objectives that are clear and concise enough to drive instruction and evaluation. Overextending the consortium will produce ambiguous content, too general to effectively guide either instruction or evaluation.

Lack of Consistency in Scope and Sequence

If the participating schools use different learning materials, resources, and technology, it is very difficult to create consistency in scope and sequence. One option is to base the scope and sequence decisions on a "majority rules" concept, creating winners and losers. That is not a good idea in curriculum because buy-in is lost. A second option is to disregard the learning materials in creating the curriculum design. The end result will be noncongruence between the curriculum design and the learning materials. If teachers are forced to choose between the curriculum document and the learning materials, they will choose the learning materials.

Lack of Ownership or Responsiveness by Teachers

Teachers who are forced to participate in curriculum consortiums that do not match their school's educational philosophy or learning materials, resources, and technology will not respond effectively in curriculum implementation. For example, if a language arts teacher from a school that emphasizes interdisciplinary curriculum based on a whole language philosophy is participating in a consortium that is designing a language arts curriculum based on a grammatical, reading book approach (also known as an anthology or basal text approach), the chances of creating ownership and responsiveness from this teacher are lacking.

Lack of Use in the Classroom

If the consortium has been overextended, teachers in the participating schools who are incompatible in educational philosophy or learning materials, resources, and technology will use avoidance behaviors and techniques that will lead to a lack of implementation of the curriculum design. It is incredible to think that such a state of affairs could exist in schools. But it does because too many curriculum consortiums are based on geography-, governance-, or purchasing-driven combinations.

Reasons for Curriculum Consortia

In view of all the warnings about the dangers of overextending curriculum consortia, the impression may be left that curriculum consortia are not a good idea. Quite to the contrary, they are a good idea for the following reasons.

Teacher Content Expertise

In small educational settings, there are schools with only one or two teachers implementing the curriculum in a grade level or subject area. In other settings, there are no teachers with experience in a certain grade level or subject area. In all educational settings, the level of content expertise among the teachers varies. In these situations, curriculum consortiums are of great benefit to the schools. Curriculum consortia allow synergy to take place within each curriculum being developed. The level of content expertise for each curriculum development in each participating school is equal to the teacher with the greatest expertise. In many cases, a synergy effect is produced, resulting in a product far superior in quality to any that could have been produced in isolation by any of the members of the curriculum group.

One of the biggest criticisms of local curriculum development is that schools constantly "reinvent the wheel." Consortia can prevent this practice. More important, consortia promote what Deming refers to as "profound knowledge."[6] This concept holds that any school or organization, regardless of its characteristics, will eventually reach its maximum potential in knowledge and will need to reach outside the organization to continue to grow intellectually. Curriculum consortia provide a delivery system for profound knowledge and thus continuous improvement in curriculum design and implementation.

Curriculum consortia allow teachers to learn from each other, to see how other schools are approaching curriculum design and implementation, and to increase their potential in each development by utilizing the best knowledge from the consortium. This is best illustrated when a state, rather than an independent schools or a school district, develops the curriculum and has a larger pool of expert teachers to participate in the curriculum process. Consortia help to keep schools from becoming too insular and provincial. Allowing teachers and schools to develop their knowledge of the gaps in their understanding will allow them to recognized curricular needs that otherwise would escape them. They are one of the best teacher development tools available for content and pedagogy growth.

Cost Reduction

Reducing costs is not the main reason for forming consortia, but it is a valuable by-product. If the volume of curriculum development can be increased without sacrificing quality and productivity, the resulting cost saving is worth pursuing. Primarily, costs are reduced because consortia cut down on administrative and leadership personnel. Are the decisions driven by curriculum or cost?

Using Curriculum Specialists More Effectively

As previously mentioned, consortia spread the influence of the best practitioners over more school districts and beyond, and thus increase their impact on curriculum design and implementation.

ALTERNATIVE APPROACHES
TO CURRICULUM DEVELOPMENT

Unfortunately, some school districts are going to be forced into curriculum consortia where the participating schools are not compatible in educational philosophy and learning materials, resources, and technology. Political, financial, as well as governance issues and practices will force them into these consortia without viable options for alternatives. If this is the situation, the schools could use the following process to maximize the opportunities and minimize the weaknesses of an incongruent curriculum consortium.

1. Comprehensive content development at the consortium level: This step may be implemented at the state, regional, or local level as learning standards are developed. In this initial step, emphasis and concentration should not be on consensus but on comprehensiveness. This step is often referred to as the creation of an objective bank or a model. Individual members of the consortium should take special care to ensure that standards, goals, objectives, or learning outcomes required by their school district be included within the bank or model. Some qualitative decisions need to be made at this level. Even though the product is only a working model, and not a final curriculum design, all content included should be defensible and based on sound curriculum thinking. This step could best be described as suggestive and comprehensive.

2. Adaptation at the appropriate level (the highest level at which educational philosophy and learning materials, resources, and technology are compatible): This step may be implemented at a regional or local level. It may be any number of districts, or perhaps only one. The key question is at what level is compatibility in educational philosophy and learning materials, resources, and technology reached? When that is determined, this adaptation step should begin. This step could best be described as prescriptive and selective.

This alternative approach to curriculum consortia is presented only because the wheels of change in governance structure work slowly. Therefore, some schools will have to continue functioning in curriculum consortia that are not compatible in educational philosophy and learning materials, resources, and technology. This approach wastes resources and creates additional processes that are not necessary in compatible consortia.

This alternative approach should not be necessary in the long term. With vast technological, synchronous communication available today, distance will no longer be a legitimate constraint to forming curriculum consortia based on common educational philosophy and learning resources. For example, schools that share a specific curriculum, purpose, or ideology, such as religious, Montessori, or other commonly oriented schools can develop curricular consortia and meet virtually.

This society has long accepted the notion that school communities are unique in demographic makeup and mission. Geographical curriculum consortia are not the delivery system best equipped to help these school systems meet their potential in curriculum design and delivery. However, consortia based on common educational philosophy and resources have the potential to network many educational agencies for the purpose of maximizing their curriculum design and implementation potential.

Selecting Teacher Representatives
for Curriculum Development

Teachers are selected to participate in curriculum development in any of five ways. Four are within control of the school administration:

1. Accepting volunteers
2. Rotating membership
3. Peer selection
4. Administrative selection

The fifth selection method is union or professional organization selection. In this case, the administration is not directly involved in the selection.

When choosing the correct method of selection, a factor that should be considered is what has evolved in the past in relation to teachers serving on curriculum developments. For example, which selection methods have been used the most? Which have been the most successful? What is the general attitude among teachers as to how this process should be accomplished? Most important of all, what existing relationships among the teaching staff, if ignored, would seriously hamper the selection process? Evolvement is not a selection process, but what has happened in the past does affect which selection processes should be used in the present and future.

Each of the selection methods has advantages and disadvantages. Following is a discussion of each method of selection and recommendations as to when it should be used.

Accepting Volunteers

The advantages of the volunteer method are as follows:

• People who volunteer are interested in the project. The motives for this interest may vary. The motive could be political, economic, educational, or organizational. For example, a teacher desires to share effective instructional practices by posting their lesson plans on the district's online curriculum document. Regardless of the motivation, it can be assumed that a commitment of some kind is involved.
• The use of volunteers is an open, democratic process.
• Accepting volunteers eliminates the need for a formal selection process.

Here are some disadvantages of this method:

- The people with the least amount of competence in the curriculum development may volunteer, thus negatively affecting the quality of the product.
- Calling for volunteers may seem to indicate that the role is not very important; the implication is that anyone is acceptable.

Recommendation for use: Using volunteers for curriculum development is feasible when the group from which the volunteers come is made up of people comparable in ability in relation to the curriculum being developed. In other words, everyone is acceptable. This means that the quality of the process and the product will not be significantly affected positively or negatively by which teachers serve as representatives for the staff.

When these conditions are present, the volunteer method may be the most desirable one because it produces an interested participant. Also, it is democratic in nature, and the use of democratic processes when possible is good for rapport and morale.

Rotating Membership

The advantages of the rotation method are as follows:

- By rotating membership on curriculum committees, all possible participants can eventually be involved in curriculum development. The more that people are involved in curriculum development, the more they tend to use the curriculum documents produced by the curriculum development process. Therefore, rotating membership has the desirable effect of increasing involvement, ownership, and responsiveness.
- Rotating eliminates the need for selection. That is a strength in itself because selection is often a controversial process.

Here are some disadvantages of this method:

- The biggest problem with rotating membership on curriculum committees is continuity. The degree of the problem will vary, but the problem will always be present. If rotation is used, the curriculum leader can assume that two things will occur: First, to ensure continuity, a great deal of attention must be given to the communication process. Second, the curriculum development process will take longer, because each time membership is rotated additional time must be set aside to update new members on the project.
- Rotating membership seems to assume that all eligible participants have equal ability to serve. Such an assumption may be erroneous.

Recommendation for use: Rotating membership on curriculum committees should be used when the process goals are more important than the product goals. Use when involvement is more important than continuity or efficiency. Always expect rotation membership to increase the time needed to achieve the goal. Rotation should be used when all the eligible participants have the ability to serve at an acceptable competence level. Examples of when rotation could be used to advantage are when the teaching staff is suffering from burnout and when the problems are instructionally related, not due to poor curriculum content or design. Rotation would address the problem of lack of responsiveness and ownership.

Peer Selection

The advantages of peer selection are as follows:

- It places power and control at the teacher level, thus increasing the likelihood of teacher ownership and responsiveness.
- It may make it easier for the teacher chosen to get cooperation from the rest of the staff on gathering input and feedback.

Here are some disadvantages of this method:

- The group may select representatives for the wrong reasons, for example, because of friendship, apathy, or financial rewards.
- The peer selection method assumes that the group members know the kind of leadership and representation they need. In some instances, this may not be true.

Recommendation for use: The peer selection process is highly recommended under the following conditions:

- When the teaching staff is mature and experienced
- When the teaching staff is committed to the importance of curriculum development
- When the teaching staff is knowledgeable concerning the curriculum development

Administrative Selection

The advantages of administrative selection are as follows:

- Administrative selection tends to legitimize the selection, thus giving it significance. Since the lack of a significant place within the school power

structure is a curriculum problem, administrative selection of teacher representation is helpful in overcoming this organizational dilemma.
- Administrators should know who the best-qualified person is.

Here are some disadvantages of administrative selection:

- As with all administrative decisions, this one may negatively affect group cooperation if the group feels the selection was based on politics rather than reason and logic.
- If the administrator is not knowledgeable about curriculum or the characteristics of the staff, using this method will be a mistake. This decision should be based on expertise. If the administrator does not have the expertise needed, this selection process is flawed.

Recommendation for use: Administrative selection should be used when volunteerism, rotation, or peer selection is not feasible.

THE ROLE OF EVOLVEMENT IN SELECTING TEACHER PARTICIPANTS FOR CURRICULUM DEVELOPMENT

When a teaching staff works together for any significant amount of time, curriculum leaders emerge. The behavior of the group members will indicate the confidence they have in this person. They will turn to the curriculum leaders for guidance when curriculum questions arise. For example, a teacher is highly skilled in integrating technology into the classroom, and the curriculum committee is creating an instructional technology framework to enhance the curriculum guide. When the issue of representation surfaces, the teaching staff will turn to the evolved leader for direction. The group will use the identified leader as its representative in a formal or informal manner—formally if the evolved leader is selected or informally if the leader is not selected.

Therefore, the curriculum leader of the school should be cognizant of the evolved curriculum leaders within the teaching staff and the circumstances, such as subject areas or grade levels, where they are perceived by their peers to be the leader.

When the administration demonstrates awareness of the evolvement process within a school, cooperation from the staff will probably be high because the group has chosen the leader or representative through its own processes. This evolvement has been accomplished through the group's own informal structure without any guidance or coercion. Therefore, the person chosen is the true leader in this curriculum area.

If the selection process is not going to choose the evolved leader, the administrator must communicate with that person to ensure his or her cooperation with whatever method of selection is going to be used. To not do so is to ignore the evolvement process, which would be a mistake. Remember, the entire selection process is to ensure good representation during the project and to increase the likelihood of ownership and responsiveness.

Keep in mind that the evolvement of true staff leaders may not have had time to take place in all situations. In these instances, evolvement is not an issue in teacher selection for curriculum development. But if evolvement has occurred, then it becomes a first step in the process. It is useful in determining who the most competent teachers are for a particular curriculum development. If the evolvement process has been observed closely by the curriculum leader, the information gathered will improve the teacher selection process.

Working with Teacher Unions on the Selection Process

In some school districts, the collective bargaining process has made the teacher's union the decision maker regarding which teachers are selected to represent the staff on curriculum developments. In these situations, the administrator charged with curriculum development should work diligently to establish communication and rapport with the union officials on this important decision. What must be communicated are the advantages, disadvantages, and recommended use for each of the methods. Hopefully, through effective dialogue, the principles outlined in this discussion will serve as the basis for selection regardless of whether the school administration or the union is in charge of the decision.

Developing an Effective Learning Community/Team in the Curriculum Development Workshop Setting

When people work together in teams, certain group and individual feelings and behaviors are predictable. The curriculum facilitator must be aware of how these feelings and behaviors will influence the curriculum development process, especially the workings within the curriculum development sessions or workshops. If curriculum workshops are conducted as if team dynamics issues will not surface, the dialogue that occurs in the workshops will be superficial. Therefore, the decisions made in the workshop will also be superficial. For the curriculum workshop to achieve quality, three basic team dynamics issues must be clarified to the satisfaction of each participant:

1. Personal identity on the team: Each participant would make the following statements to describe their personal identity on the team:

   - "I have something to offer this project; knowledge, experience."
   - "I have the motivation and skills to contribute to this curriculum development."

2. Relationships among team members: Each participant would make the following statements to describe the relationships among team members:

- "I can work with these people."
- "I can be open and honest with them."
- "I can disagree with them without destroying the working relationship."
- "I respect these people. They can contribute also."

3. Identity with the organization: Each participant would make the following statements to describe how they identify with the organization.

- "This curriculum development is important to the school."
- "I want this school to be a good one." "I want to participate in this curriculum development because it will improve our school."

This discussion on how to develop an effective learning community or team for curriculum development is couched in the long-standing works of M. Scott Peck[7] and Bruce Wayne Tuckman.[8]

The approaches used by these authors are quite similar. Taken in tandem, they aptly describe the feelings and behaviors that dominate teams or learning communities when embarking upon a project such as curriculum development. There are subtle differences between the authors with one additional stage, Adjourning, in Tuckman's research; see table 4.1 for a comparison of their terminology and descriptors. The stages and phases described in the following paragraphs will collectively form the basis for recommendations regarding curriculum leadership and facilitation.

CHARACTERISTICS OF STAGES AND PHASES

Stage 1: Forming/Pseudocommunity (Peck)

Feelings:

- Excitement, anticipation, optimism
- Pride in being chosen

Table 4.1. Stages of Team Growth

Development (Tuckman)	Phases of Community (Peck)
1. Forming	I. Pseudocommunity
2. Storming	II. Chaos
3. Norming	III. Trust, Emptying, Listening
4. Performing	IV. True Community
5. Adjourning	

- Initial, tentative, attachment to team
- Suspicion, fear, anxiety

Behaviors:

- Arguing among members
- Defensiveness and competition
- Questioning wisdom of those selected and appointed
- Establishing unrealistic goals
- Perceived "pecking order"
- Increased tension
- Storming/breakdown
- Basic survival behaviors
- New leaders emerge from the group
- Great success occurs
- New members contribute
- Someone says the "unspeakable" thing
- Any channel discussion (discussion among team members not shared with the entire group)
- Unmanaged personal conflict occurs
- "Pairing off" by cliques/factions
- Fight/flight behavior
- Very frightening to the system
- Highly reptilian in nature
- A defining moment will occur (The tum will define itself in the process.)
- Continuous storming/chaos looks back to forming/pseudocommunity for solutions
- Going back and forth between storming/chaos and forming/pseudo produces burnout

Stage 2: Storming/Chaos

Feelings:

- Resistance to the task and different approaches
- Sharp fluctuations in attitude

Behaviors:

- Arguing among members
- Defensiveness and competition
- Questioning wisdom of those selected and appointed
- Establishing unrealistic goals

- Perceived "pecking order"
- Increased tension
- Storming/breakdown
- Basic survival behaviors
- New leaders emerge from the group
- Great success occurs
- New members contribute
- Someone says the "unspeakable" thing
- Any channel discussion (discussion among team members not shared with the entire group)
- Unmanaged personal conflict occurs
- "Pairing off" by cliques/factions
- Fight/flight behavior
- Very frightening to the system
- Highly reptilian in nature
- A defining moment will occur (The tum will define itself in the process.)
- Continuous storming/chaos looks back to forming/pseudocommunity for solutions
- Going back and forth between storming/chaos and forming/pseudo produces burnout

Stage 3: Norming/Trust, Emptying, Listening

Feelings:

- New ability to criticize constructively
- Acceptance of membership in team
- Relief everything is going to work out

Behaviors:

- An attempt to achieve harmony
- More friendliness, confiding, sharing
- Sense of team cohesion
- Establishing and maintaining rules and boundaries
- Norming
- Voices being heard
- Communication
- Facilitation
- Conflict resolution
- Understanding
- Respect—I see you for the first time

- Emptying file
- Listening is used
- Goal of this phase is completeness
- Demographics (accepting of differences/nobody dies)
- But is changed to and

Stage 4: Performing/True Community

Feelings:

- Insights into personal and group processes
- Understanding of each other's strengths and weaknesses
- Satisfaction with the team's progress

Behaviors:

- Constructive self-change
- Ability to prevent or work through group problems
- Close attachment to the team
- Values and goals are different
- Differences are valued
- "Help me understand to see what you see"
- Conflict managed; based on issues, not personalities
- Defines itself by differences
- Honors diversity
- High performance-growth, development, thinking occur

Stage 5: Adjourning (Tuckman)

Feelings:

- Satisfaction in the accomplishment
- Sadness in the loss of relationships
- Sense of loss
- Uncertain about the future

Behaviors:

- Working toward completion of the project
- Moving off into different directions
- Disengagement of relationships
- Less focused on the task
- Less productivity
- Disbandment

RECOMMENDATIONS FOR CURRICULUM LEADERSHIP AND FACILITATION

It is not enough just to know the stages of team development. A curriculum leader must know how to facilitate the team through the team dynamics issues and the stages of team development. Following are suggestions and recommendations for the curriculum leader/facilitator.

I. Addressing the Team Dynamics Issues

   A. Personal identity on the team: Make sure they know how and why they were chosen to represent their teaching staff on this curriculum development.

- Specify the expertise you feel they bring to the curriculum development process.
- Give them the opportunity to describe the forces for and against their participation in the curriculum development.
- Give them the opportunity to express the strengths and weaknesses they bring to the process.

   B. Relationship among the team members: Expect the four phases/stages of community/team development to occur.

- Don't let the team drift back and forth between forming and storming. Force them to move toward norming.
- Structure interpersonal communication activities early in the workshop, so that forming can begin as soon as possible.
- Give them as much information about each other as possible so relationships can begin to form as soon as possible.

   C. Identity with the organization: In the workshop, discuss the importance of the curriculum development to the school.

- Show how it fits the mission of the school.
- Show how it could be or is making a difference in school quality, including student achievement.
- Show your commitment to the participants by using quality time for curriculum development and giving them the clerical/technical assistance they need to accomplish their tasks as teacher representatives to the curriculum development process.
- Connect curriculum development to student achievement and assessment.

II. Getting the Team through Forming/Pseudocommunity

    A. Make no substantive decisions about content or format.

- Have a comfortable environment to build on the excitement, anticipation, and optimism that accompanies this stage.
- Take time for team-building activities.
- Clarify roles to help relieve suspicion, fear, and anxiety.
- Clearly define the task.
- Keep the group focused without being overly dominant.
- Address complaints and barriers without being antagonistic.
- Conduct the workshop away from the school buildings where the teacher participants work.
- Make sure substitute teachers have been hired well in advance so that teachers participating in the curriculum development can plan adequately for their absence from the classroom.
- Relieve participating teachers from all other obligations for the day.
- Foster and encourage philosophical or abstract comments about the curriculum development.
- Remain positive even when negativity seems to permeate the process.
- Don't take over the decision-making process when conflict occurs.
- Allow conflicts among the participants to resolve themselves without your interference if possible. Intervene only as a last resort.

III. Getting the Team through Storming/Chaos

    A. Keep your cool.

- Don't let them establish unrealistic goals.
- Ensure balanced input.
- Keep discussion focused on issues.
- If cliques develop, make sure they don't shut off discussion.
- Revisit interpersonal communications techniques if necessary.
- Build on defining moments when a participant takes a risk and survives by calling attention to the team's progress.
- Do not let them drift back to forming; remind them that progress can be made only by continuing to strive for norming.
- When critiquing becomes constructive in nature, allow substantive content decision making to begin. (Note: Follow this principle at any stage in which constructive critiquing occurs.)

IV. Allowing the Team to Norm

    A. Monitor ground rules and boundaries.

- Encourage the team to make substantive content and format decisions.
- Utilize the individual strengths of the team members.

- Facilitate! Facilitate! Facilitate! But don't make decisions. Let the team make decisions through consensus.

V. Assisting the Team during Performing/True Community

   A. Give task-relevant feedback: Allow sufficient dialogue to accommodate insights and high-performance characteristics such as personal growth, development, critical thinking, and creativity.

VI. Assisting the Team during Adjournment

   A. Address the transition.

   - Ensure completion of the product.
   - Evaluate the team's process and product.
   - Identify lessons learned for future work.
   - Emphasize gratitude.
   - Celebrate achievement and contributions to formally end the team's existence.

The Planning or Initial Workshop

The initial session or workshop for any curriculum development, herein referred to as a planning workshop, should have two purposes:

- To develop a tentative curriculum document, usually a course of study, or an instructional resource guide
- To establish rules and procedures for gathering staff input on the tentative curriculum document developed in the planning workshop

COMPONENTS AND STRATEGIES FOR A SUCCESSFUL PLANNING WORKSHOP

The success of a planning workshop depends on various components and strategies. Some of these are described in the following paragraphs.

Schedule Curriculum Workshops during Quality Time

There are three requirements for quality time to be in effect. First, the workshop must be held during the regular school day or during summer vacation. If the workshop occurs during the regular school day, no teacher stipend is necessary. If the workshop takes place during summer vacation, the teacher should receive a reasonable stipend, that is, a professional wage.

Second, the workshop must take place away from the school buildings of the teacher participants. It is vital that the participants give their entire intellectual attention to the curriculum development. If they are in the school building where they teach, there is a greater chance of them being asked to take care of a school problem. This time and energy diverts their attention from the curriculum development.

Third, the workshop must be planned in advance so that the participants have had time to plan the instructional day with the substitute teacher. This, of course, increases the chances of the students having a productive day. In relation to the curriculum development, it will help ensure that the teachers can give their full attention to the curriculum development.

In summary, these strategies are designed to ensure that, for this day, curriculum development is the natural work function for the participants. If all these strategies are in place, the teacher participants are emotionally and intellectually free to concentrate on the task at hand-producing a quality tentative curriculum document.

Make Effective Use of a Working Model

A curriculum-working model is a document (hard copy or an electronic version) that is used as a starting or reference point for the curriculum development process. The working model allows the curriculum worker to accept, revise and accept, and add or delete content without having to write learning objectives and other content from scratch. Using working models increases efficiency, saves time and energy for debate and discussion, produces consistency of language, and provides a format for presenting all relevant data needed to help teachers make good decisions about curriculum content.

Working Models for Curriculum Development

When a school has no current curriculum development document, an external working model will be needed. Sources of working models for curriculum development include the following:

- Other school districts—with similar philosophy, books, resources, and technology—that have recently developed a successful curriculum
- Research-based data and information on the curricular topic
- University curriculum reference libraries
- State education departments' curriculum websites
- State, national, or accrediting associations that are relevant

Sources of working models for curriculum revision include the following:

- The current curriculum document if it has been evaluated and deemed worthy to be utilized as a working model
- Curriculum evaluation or audit results
- Evaluation results from instructional team findings and recommendations
- State, national, or accrediting associations that are relevant

Working Model Format

The working model should be in a format that allows workshop participants to indicate scope and sequence decisions efficiently and effectively. Figures 4.3 and 3.4 illustrate the directions for developing student learning standards, or objectives, and one page from a sample working model. In figure 4.4, note the blank columns after objective 7; they are provided for the curriculum team to include additional desired learning objectives.

The working model should not dictate decisions about scope and sequence. It is a tool to assist the curriculum team in making the right decisions (effectiveness), and in making them as quickly and conveniently as possible (efficiency).

BASING CURRICULUM DECISIONS ON DATA, NOT GUESSWORK

Although the aim of curriculum process is to produce teacher ownership and responsiveness, curriculum development and revision should begin with an analysis of the current performance of students. The entire curriculum process from beginning to end is designed to ensure congruency of the instructional program with the planned curriculum.

However, the process, whether it is development of student objectives or instructional resources or revision, should begin with an analysis of the current performance of the students. Most assuredly, teacher expertise, expressed through the pursuit of consensus, is vital to the process. But before pursuing this consensus, data and information about the strengths and weaknesses of the current curriculum as measured by student performance should be a prerequisite to any discussion of curriculum content.

If the data reveals success in certain content areas, such data are an indication that the current learning objectives in that content area should remain relatively unchanged. If data reveal failure, then significant thought must be given to why and how it could be corrected.

WORKING MODEL
Directions to Teacher Consultants
SOCIAL STUDIES (S.S.)

This is a working model to assist in the development of an S.S. course of study. On each page of this paper, you will find objectives and sub-objectives within a major category of an S.S. program. Your task is to:

Step 1: Read and make sure you understand the objective and sub-objectives
Step 2: Add to the list of sub-objectives any further objectives that you have or would want to have in your program. When you have written your additions on the pages provided, number each one and then proceed to Step 3.
Step 3: Read each objective and sub-objective and decide (by placing a check in the appropriate column) whether the objective is Essential, Important, or Not Appropriate. (For those you have added, the decision is between Essential and Important.)

Essential: Means that the objective or sub-objective should receive top priority and must be in the course of study for the course of study to be complete. Essential objectives must be approved by all as essential.
Important: Means that the objective or sub-objective should be included in the course of study if time permits but will not replace the essential objectives or sub-objectives.
Not Appropriate: Means either of two things: (1) The objective or sub-objectives should not be included in a course of study. (2) The objective or sub-objective is not taught at these grade levels but may be appropriate at another level. (Remember that only one check is appropriate for each objective or sub- objective. Do not check both Essential and Important.)

Step 4: Now look at the grade-level columns. Your task is to check the grade level at which the sub-objective should be taught by introduction or reinforcement.

Definitions:

Introduced: At what time and in what grade level do you first deal with this sub-objective as an intentional part of the instruction? (When do you first try to teach the sub-objective?)
Reinforced: Means, in this paper, that by direct instructional activities you come back and go over or extend the learning about the sub-objectives. It does not mean the informal and ongoing practice of a skill that would naturally occur in the ordinary activities of school. For instance, following oral directions is a listening skill that is practiced continually. We want to know where you intentionally introduce the teaching of the skill and where you repeat (reinforce), with actual instructional activities, the skill.

Step 5: When you have completed Steps 1 through 4 on major objectives, you have finished with that objective. Go to the next objective and begin with Step 1 again.

Figure 4.3.   A Social Studies Working Model

	Essential	Important	Delete	Kindergarten	1st Grade	2nd Grade	3rd Grade
Listening Skills Show that you can follow directions.							
1. Follow directions for drawing pictures.							
Edit							
2. Follow directions indicating a sentence to the teacher describing a picture, an object, or an experience.							
Edit							
3. Follow directions in making a copy of your name from a model.							
Edit							
4. Follow directions in arranging pictures and objects in a predetermined order.							
Edit							
5. Follow directions for playing games.							
Edit							
6. Follow directions in completing worksheets.							
Edit							
7. Follow oral directions involving several steps.							
Edit							
8. Additions							

Figure 4.4. An Assessment Working-Model Form

This analysis should be used to discuss both scope (what is taught) and sequence (when and in what order). Curriculum problems could be caused by either scope or sequence; therefore, both scope and sequence should be analyzed. Consensus should be used as the basic decision-making process in curriculum. However, consensus cannot be used to make decisions that are contrary to the data on student achievement.

The following data is shared with teacher-consultants either prior to the planning (initial) workshop or at the beginning of the initial workshop: current student performance results on standardized tests, other performance measures, critical success factors, key features, management and improvement systems, and improvement goals.

DIALOGUE VERSUS PREPARATORY
CURRICULUM PROCESS MODEL

In the dialogue model, the planning workshop would be used for the introduction of the working model. The teacher-consultants would not have seen the working model, such as the standards, before coming to the planning workshop. The rationale for the dialogue model is that it reduces the chances of the teachers coming to the workshop with fixed positions on what the curriculum content should be. Thus, after the presentation of the data, the group immediately launches into dialogue about scope and sequence focused around the working model.

In the preparatory model, the working model would be sent to the teacher-consultants before the planning workshop. They would be able to study the proposed working model and come to preliminary decisions about either the learning objectives and scope and sequence or instructional resources depending on the goal of the curriculum process. With this model, there is no fear of individual fixed positions hindering the quality of the curriculum development effort.

RECOMMENDED USE OF EACH CURRICULUM
PROCESS MODEL

The decision about which model to use should be made after looking at four important questions. They are the following:

• Is the curriculum process a revision or a development? A revision favors the use of the preparatory model. A development favors a dialogue model. In using a revision, the teachers will bring fixed positions to the planning workshop; they have already formed opinions about the curriculum document through their experience in implementing the curriculum in their classrooms. To expect them to begin dialogue about the curriculum without an opinion of its merits is unreasonable.

On the other hand, curriculum development favors the dialogue model because the group is beginning without a history, and thus without data. Therefore, as the curriculum leader, you do not want the teachers to come to the initial workshop with preconceived notions that are not based on data, literature, or research.

- Is the current curriculum successful? Evaluation of the curriculum and instructional resources should be based on student achievement data, curriculum audits, audits, and feedback from the teachers who have implemented the curriculum in the classroom.

When the current curriculum has been successful, the preparatory model allows the group to revise the curriculum or focus their effort on aligning instruction with the curriculum in the most efficient manner. Past success means that fewer changes are likely, or needed. Therefore, the preparatory model will save time and resources by determining areas of consensus before the planning workshop occurs.

When the current curriculum has not been successful, the dialogue model allows the group to initiate the curriculum revision process by focusing on the data and the areas needing improvement, which it will point out.

- What is the level of consensus among the teaching staff? If the consensus is high, then fixed positions will be a strength. Therefore, the preparatory model would be appropriate. If consensus is low, that is a strong indicator that the dialogue model would be the best choice.
- Which is the major emphasis of the project: the product or the process! Sometimes a curriculum project is designed to improve the communications, interpersonal relationships, and team building as much as it is to improve the curriculum design. In those cases, the dialogue model will be more likely to achieve these goals. If the emphasis is solely on producing a quality document, then the preparatory model best serves this aim.

Strategies for Gathering Staff Input

To perform this phase of the curriculum process, teacher-consultants must be skilled in conducting small-group discussions. Specifically, the teacher-consultant must have the skill to create maximum group input and make consensus decisions.

The goal of the staff input phase is to ensure that every teacher who will be implementing the planned curriculum has the opportunity to contribute input. To assure that this input strengthens the process, the teacher-consultant must attempt to replicate the planning workshop as closely as possible. It is important to relate to the staff not only what was decided but also why and how. In addition, the input phase should use the same dialogue style that was used in the planning workshop.

It must be done through personal interaction. To immediately use online surveys, checklists, or other forms of nonverbal communication would destroy the dialogue principle upon which the process is based. It would prevent the staff from hearing the rationale of the teacher-consultants. Thus the staff members would be making decisions without the full benefit of the expertise of those teachers who have already been identified as highly competent in this academic field.

The teacher-consultant should have copies of the tentative curriculum document that was developed at the planning workshop. Each staff member should have a hard copy or access to their own electronic copy. If the preparatory model is being used, the tentative curriculum document should be sent to the teachers before the staff input session. If the dialogue model is being used, the tentative curriculum document should be introduced at the actual session.

When the teacher-consultant leaves the staff input session, the consultant provides the input needed for the feedback workshop.

Feedback Workshops

The goal of the feedback workshop is to finalize, or move toward conclusion of, the curriculum document. The teacher-consultants come to the feedback workshop with the input they have gathered from their staffs. The same decision-making process is used: decisions are based on data and consensus.

If the participants cannot come to consensus on content or sequence, a second staff input session is called for. The process of going back and forth between feedback workshops and staff input continues until consensus is reached, thus finalizing the curriculum document.

THE PLANNING WORKSHOP AGENDA

Here is a typical planning workshop agenda.

8:00 a.m.–8:45 a.m.	Introductions, Purpose, and Human Development Activities
8:45 a.m.–9:15 a.m.	Presentation of Working Model and Evaluation Data
9:15 a.m.–12 noon	For developing Learning Standards—Content Development Philosophy, Scope, Sequence of Learning Objectives, etc. For developing Curriculum

Guides—Instructional Development Philosophy, Best
Teaching Practices, Model Lessons, Resources, etc.

Noon–1:00 p.m.   Lunch
1:00 p.m.–3:00 p.m.   Continue Content Development
3:00 p.m.–5:00 p.m.   Input

SOME TIPS ON HOW TO CONDUCT
CURRICULUM WORKSHOPS

Once states, school districts, county schools, or independent schools decide
the purpose of the curriculum work, workshops can begin. The following tips
on conducting curriculum workshops include recommendations for the best
environment, human development activities, and facilitation strategies.

Environment

1. Hold the workshop away from individual schools and during quality time.
2. Make sure the environment is comfortable. The room should have the following characteristics:

   • Comfortable work seats
   • Circular seating arrangement
   • Tables with room for participants to spread out their working model,
     charts, and papers
   • Good acoustics

3. Serve appropriate refreshments.
4. Provide desk nametags and necessary technology.

HUMAN DEVELOPMENT ACTIVITIES

In many instances, the teacher-consultants will not know one another. Therefore, some preliminary activities to create an atmosphere conducive to effective curriculum decision making are needed. Human development activities
are designed to produce openness and honesty among the participants. An
additional benefit is that they allow workshop attendees to identify the specific
expertise of the individual teacher-consultants. This information could prove
beneficial during the decision-making process. Many different activities can
be used. The literature refers to them as "icebreakers," but in curriculum workshops, they are more than that. They help set the stage for the day's dialogue.

FACILITATION TIPS

- Don't spend too much time agreeing to agree. Allow this to the point that the participants are reinforcing one another, thus strengthening the consensus. However, don't allow it to dominate the conversation until there is no time for debate where there is disagreement or lack of consensus. Remember, the purpose of the workshop is curriculum decision making.
- Interpret silence to mean agreement. Curriculum subject areas have areas of almost universal agreement. For example, in math, many computational skills are a given. When going through these content areas, present them and take silence as agreement. Don't make the attendees grunt their assent for six hours.
- Don't read each objective or instructional idea from the working model. Indicate the number, refer to the key words or phrases, let the teachers read and think, and then discuss.
- Constantly emphasize that curriculum decisions should be based on what ought to be, not what is. Do not allow decisions on specific objectives to be based on whether or not they are currently being taught. The pertinent questions are: Should it be taught? How should it best be taught? The facilitator must continually emphasize this point.

Intended Process Outcomes

The processes described in this chapter are intended to produce the following outcomes:

- Curriculum content decisions will be based on student achievement data. The data includes the following
  - Classroom performances (portfolios, papers, projects, etc.)
  - Student performance on curriculum-based assessments
  - Student performance on standardized tests
  - Teacher evaluation
  - Follow-up studies
- In content decisions not mandated by internal or external authorities, consensus decision making will be utilized. The challenge of curriculum design is to perform the function so that the design will be implemented in the classroom. If all teachers affected by the curriculum design are involved in its development, the chances of this occurring are increased. The integration and congruence between curriculum and instruction should be the ultimate aim of every school's curriculum design and the processes used to accomplish its fulfillment.

NOTES

1. Elementary Secondary Education Act (ESEA), http://education.laws.com/elementary-and-secondary-education-actLaw.com (accessed 2017).

2. A Nation at Risk (1983), https://www2.ed.gov/pubs/NatAtRisk/risk.html (accessed April 1983).

3. Richard W. Riley (1995), The Improving America's Schools Act of 1994. https://www2.ed.gov/offices/OESE/archives/legislation/ESEA/brochure/iasa-bro.html (accessed September 1995).

4. Alyson Klein (2017), The Every Student Succeeds Act: An ESSA Overview. https://www.edweek.org/ew/issues/every-student-succeeds-act/ (accessed March 31, 2016).

5. Edward Graham (2013), "A Nation at Risk Turns 30: Where Did It Take Us?" NEA Today, http://neatoday.org/2013/04/25/a-nation-at-risk-turns-30-where-did-it-take-us-2/ (accessed April 13, 2013).

6. W. Edwards Deming, *The New Economics for Industry, Government, and Education,* 2nd ed. (Cambridge, MA: MIT Press, 2000).

7. M. Scott Peck, *The Different Drum: Community Making and Peace* (New York: Simon & Schuster, 1987).

8. Barbara J. Streibel, Brian L. Joiner, and Peter R. Scholtes, *The Team Handbook,* Third Edition (Madison, WI: Oriel Inc., 2003).

REFERENCE

Posner, G. J., and A. N. Rudnitsky. (2005). *Course Design: A Guide to Curriculum Development for Teachers, Seventh Edition.* London, England: Pearson Education Publishing.

Chapter 5

Curriculum Decision Making

ADMINISTRATIVE DECISIONS

For a quality curriculum program to be in effect, the school administration must make three critical decisions:

- Which process will be used: backloading or frontloading?
- Which curriculum development model will be used: a preparatory model that emphasizes teacher preparation followed by dialogue on the curriculum content or a dialogue model that emphasizes immediate discussion of the curriculum content?
- How will consensus decision making be used for the entire curriculum development process?

BACKLOADING VERSUS FRONTLOADING

Frontloading is defined as a process whereby the curriculum is designed first, and then textbooks, learning materials, and technology are chosen on the basis of their congruency with the curriculum design.

Backloading is defined as a process whereby the curriculum is designed to be congruent with existing textbooks, learning materials, and technology.

From the theoretical perspective, frontloading is the preferred method. The school should determine its curriculum content without being constrained by outside forces. The school should determine its content first, and then seek materials and technology that coincide and thus enhance its chances of being successful.

In situations where frontloading is not feasible, backloading is utilized. For example, the school may not be financially able to purchase new textbooks, materials, and/or technology at the time that the curriculum is being revised or developed. Teachers have to work with what they have. In those instances, it is better to correlate with existing resources than to ignore their existence. To do so will force the classroom teacher to choose between the curriculum design and the resources available to teach the course or grade-level subject matter. The resources, that is, the textbook, learning materials, and technology, will win every time. Therefore, the curriculum designed may not become the actual curriculum or the curriculum being taught.

A second instance where backloading should be used is if the school decides that the textbooks, learning materials, and/or technology are so strong that they deserve to drive the curriculum development process.

In the current political climate, with emphasis on common core, and assessment based on state and national standards, schools have no choice but to backload the curriculum to meet outcomes that have been predetermined for them.

The point of this discussion is that a school system needs to make the decision to either frontload or backload before the curriculum development begins. This decision has tremendous impact on the entire curriculum development process.

COMPARING THE PREPARATORY
AND DIALOGUE MODELS

Both of these curriculum development models use dialogue as the basis for content decision making. The only difference in the two models is in the state of communication at the beginning of the curriculum development process.

In the preparatory model, participants have the opportunity to study the working model before coming to the planning (first) workshop. As a result, the participants tend to come to the curriculum development process with fixed positions, sometimes even advocacy positions. Therefore, the positions are difficult to dislodge. Most certainly, these fixed positions or advocacy positions will form the basis for the initial discussion on curricular content.

In the dialogue model, the participants will not have the chance to study the working model before coming to the first planning workshop. Therefore, they will not have had the opportunity to form fixed or advocacy positions, thus centering the initial discussion more on the content of the working model. This is not to suggest that fixed or advocacy positions may not arise during the curriculum development process. The important factor is that fixed positions will not be as significant in the initial dialogue.

In both models, consensus decision making will be used. However, the consensus discussion will begin at different points in the two models due to the varying methods of initial communication. Once the initial discussion and decision-making process has occurred, the two models will look more and more alike as dialogue becomes the mode of curricular activity. In some cases, the end result will be the same. In other cases, the result will be different. So, if different results are probable, serious thought should be given as to which model of communication and decision making will produce the best-quality curriculum development process and product.

SELECTING THE APPROPRIATE MODEL

There is no right and wrong model. Neither is there a rank order in relation to quality. The proper selection depends on certain criteria present in the schools involved in the curriculum development.

The following factors should be considered in selecting the dialogue or preparatory model.

Note: Consider all factors before deciding on the appropriate model to use.

Determining Which Model to Use

The following questions can be addressed in determining whether the preparatory or dialogue model is most appropriate for use.

What Is the Level of Consensus on Content/Methodology?

High consensus level-use preparatory. If there is a high level or degree of consensus among the stakeholders concerning the current curriculum design, using the preparatory model will tend to reduce the number of workshops required to complete the curriculum process, thus making the process more efficient without the fear of losing quality. Also, since there is a high degree of consensus, the problem of fixed positions is not acute if the current curriculum design is successful.

Low level-use dialogue. If there is a low level or degree of consensus among the stakeholders concerning the current curriculum design, the dialogue model is called for. In this situation, there are many different fixed positions; using the preparatory model would only tend to entrench them. Beginning the curriculum process with dialogue, without using the preparation step, gives the consensus process a better chance of succeeding.

Is the Curriculum Process a Development or a Revision?

Unless the current curriculum design is failing, curriculum revision usually follows the preparatory model. The term *revision* indicates that there is an existing document. Through its implementation, this document has generated lots of evaluative information and data. This information and data must be processed and considered in the curriculum revision process. To ignore its presence and significance is to ignore the previous curriculum process. If a school system ignores previous curriculum efforts, it will find it difficult to get the teaching staff to take the current one seriously. Why should they?

What Is the Effect of Curriculum Alignment?

In recent decades, government agencies, both national and state, have become more involved in curriculum decision making. They have mandated testing programs, thus forcing schools to adopt and align curriculum content to match the tests. This trend has produced a curriculum process that is neither development nor revision. It is operationally defined as curriculum alignment.

That part of the curriculum that has been mandated by the state or national government is referred to as boilerplate. It is a given. There is no local decision making regarding either scope or sequence. Therefore, at the local level, schools should attempt to develop a process that will produce the most effective reaction from teachers and administrators. It is not productive for the school system to lament or be critical of the curriculum alignment process; that only increases the teachers' resentment and makes implementation more difficult. Also, if the school can create a process whereby alignment is achieved effectively, more time will be available for parts of the curriculum that are left to local decision.

Curriculum alignment occurs in both development and revision processes. The communication of the boilerplate information can best be achieved through either the dialogue or preparatory model. Since the curriculum design is predetermined, the school must concentrate on the implementation phase. The fact that the teachers were not involved in the design means that the alignment process violates all the principles of effective curriculum processes. This makes it more difficult to create commitment, ownership, and responsiveness. School curriculum leaders have to communicate to the staffs that curriculum has become a significant part of the political spectrum of schools. It is in curriculum and instruction that legislators and special interest groups have concentrated their criticism and reform efforts. What has resulted is a larger boilerplate for school curriculum.

The long-term results of the continual growth of curriculum alignment would be a state and/or a national curriculum. Most curriculum scholars oppose both state and national curriculum. That fact does not negate the need for local schools to have an effective practice for curriculum alignment. The goal of the alignment process should be to create ownership and responsiveness at the local level despite the absence of involvement in the design and content decision phases.

Assessing the Current Curriculum Document

Before deciding which model to use, dialogue or preparatory, evaluate the current curriculum design and implementation. This can be a part of a systematic needs assessment conducted by the district. This assessment, performed through a curriculum audit (to assess curriculum design) and an instructional audit (to assess curriculum implementation), should be based on the following data:

- Student test data: This analysis consists of looking at how well the students are performing on norm-referenced and criterion (i.e., curriculum)-referenced tests. This can be assessed district-wide, school-wide, by grade level, or by class.
- Student performance data: This analysis consists of outcomes of pupil performance, follow-up studies on student success levels in higher education and future employment, grade-point averages (GPAs), graduation rates, attendance figures, and enrollment figures for elective classes. This can be assessed district-wide, school-wide, by grade level, or by class.
- Feedback: This analysis consists of ongoing feedback from students, parents, colleges, and employers.
- Teacher feedback: This analysis consists of both formal and informal feedback from the teachers who have taught the curriculum.

USING CONSENSUS DECISION MAKING EFFECTIVELY

Consensus can be defined as two or more people cooperatively arriving at a decision they can support. Curriculum always involves two or more people. More important, it is imperative that all teachers who will be teaching a curriculum design be willing to support the design. Consensus offers the best chance of this occurring.

Consensus is needed by those who must act together to carry out a decision or problem. Many people act together to carry out both curriculum design and delivery. Therefore, consensus is an effective approach.

When Consensus Is Not Appropriate

The consensus model may not be appropriate for routine decisions. Teachers are too busy to go through time-consuming consensus decision making unless they are significantly affected by the decision. When this occurs, teachers usually interpret it as a weakness on the part of the leadership, and not as democratic leadership.

Consensus is not appropriate for decisions that are covered by policy and regulation. It is a moot point. Once again, teachers are too busy for rhetorical discussions on matters that are governed by policy. If the policy is bad, it may need discussion. Don't confuse it with curriculum consensus decision making, especially when given a presentation as a fait accompli.

Emergency curriculum decisions do not lend themselves to consensus. By definition, an emergency needs immediate solution. Consensus cannot occur immediately. Therefore, don't even think about using it in a crisis.

Sometimes the school system has assigned specific curriculum responsibility to a particular staff member or members. The curriculum participants should not attempt to usurp this responsibility.

Advantages of Consensus

The advantages of consensus closely coincide with the decision-making needs of curriculum design and delivery. Consensus is based on cooperating. It expresses the win-win philosophy so necessary for effective curriculum. Consensus emphasizes group unity. It also attempts, as does curriculum, to accommodate all concerns if at all possible. Consensus explores creative ideas. Creativity is the basis for continual improvement in curriculum. Perhaps most significant, consensus creates a greater commitment to implementation. In curriculum terminology, this means a greater commitment to implementing the curriculum design.

What Consensus Means to a Curriculum Development

Any curriculum development that uses consensus accepts that the following processes are taking place:

- All group members (all constituents) contribute.
- Everyone's opinions are encouraged and acknowledged.

- Differences are viewed as helpful.
- Everyone has an opportunity to express feelings about the curriculum issue at hand.
- Those who disagree express a willingness to experiment for a certain period of time.
- All members share in the final decision.
- All members agree to take responsibility for implementing the final decision.

What Consensus Does Not Mean
to a Curriculum Development

Consensus does not mean that the curriculum decisions made were unanimous votes, or that the result is everyone's first choice, or that everyone totally agrees with the decision. Table 5.1 is a comparison of majority voting versus consensus-type decision making.

Following are tips on reaching consensus when the group is seriously divided:

- Don't move to a higher level of generalization to reach consensus. Two elements of effective curriculum design are clear and valid learning objectives. To move to higher levels of generalization in order to reach consensus will tend to produce learning objectives that are too vague to have meaning in the teaching and learning process. They cannot effectively guide instruction. Let's take the example of a group of American history teachers trying to reach consensus on how to teach the military history of the Civil War. Some teachers want the students to learn the place, date, outcome, and significance of each major battle. Others only want the students to demonstrate the ability to answer questions about the military aspects of the war through personal research. Obviously, these two positions are not close to consensus. However, both groups would probably agree to this objective: Students will understand the military history of the Civil War. Theoretically, consensus has been reached. But the consensus is too general to guide instruction. Therefore, the consensus decision will not enhance the curriculum development.
- If necessary, fall back on a point made under the discussion called, "what consensus means to curriculum development." That point was: Those who

Table 5.1.   Comparison of Voting and Consensus

Voting	*Consensus*
1. Considers two points of view	1. Considers many points of view
2. Discussion divides group	2. Discussion solidifies group
3. Promotes majority and minority	3. Eliminates majority and minority
4. Fast decision and slow implementation	4. Slow decision but faster implementation

disagree express a willingness to experiment for a certain period of time. Then, based on an evaluation process, the learning objective will be revisited. There is a big difference between agreeing to something permanent and agreeing to an experiment for a definite period of time.

- Study techniques that have been devised to help a group reach consensus when dialogue has been exhausted. Three of the most commonly used techniques are multivoting, nominal group technique, and the decision matrix. All of these techniques are designed to show the group, in a nonthreatening manner, the status of the decision-making process. It shows how deeply divided the group is on the issue. Sometimes, showing the data helps to change people's position on the issue. Or, the data provides fresh information for dialogue. The curriculum facilitator should use these techniques to move the group toward consensus. The techniques should not be used in lieu of consensus. To do so would negate the entire consensus rationale for curriculum decision making.

RATIONALE FOR USING CONSENSUS DECISION MAKING IN CURRICULUM DEVELOPMENT

For curriculum design to be effectively correlated with instruction, curriculum content decisions must be made by the teachers who are responsible for teaching the planned curriculum. Using teachers as decision makers in curriculum content produces ownership and responsiveness, which are prerequisites to quality curriculum.

Second, consensus must be the decision-making process utilized in curriculum development because it is the only decision-making process that can produce a win-win situation. Acceptance of curriculum decisions must not be decided by majority vote, which creates a win-lose situation. All the teachers will be asked to implement the curriculum decisions. Therefore, all teachers should be involved in the decision-making process through consensus.

CURRICULUM CONTENT DECISIONS

Curriculum content decisions revolve around three distinctly different types of curriculum, each necessary for a quality curriculum program:

- **Boilerplate curriculum** state and federal mandates that are predetermined and not subject to consensus by the local school.
- **Locally required curriculum** learning objectives and outcomes that, by consensus, the local school has decided must be taught and assessed. This curriculum will be prescribed.

- **Elective curriculum** enrichment learning objectives that will be taught to appropriate students in addition to the boilerplate and locally required curriculum. This curriculum will be suggestive.

Boilerplate Curriculum

The boilerplate type of curriculum comes in the form of federal and state mandates. Examples are state testing in the form of proficiency tests, or state-mandated, competency-based curriculum, such as the Common Core Standards and the PARC (Partnership for Assessment of Readiness for College and Careers) or AIR (American Institute for Research) tests. Therefore, there is no decision making regarding what should be taught based on local preference. Instead, the decisions revolve around when to introduce and reinforce the mandated curriculum, and how to teach the students in order to best prepare them for the assessment.

From the curriculum perspective, the decision is the sequencing process—when to introduce, when to reinforce, and when to expect mastery. Perhaps the most important decision is an instructional one: how best to teach the mandated curriculum to achieve the best results.

Dealing with boilerplate curriculum is challenging because of the teacher ownership issue. It is harder to get the teaching staff to own and respond to boilerplate curriculum with the same zeal that they feel for the local curriculum that they helped formulate. Keep in mind how important teacher ownership and responsiveness are to successful curriculum implementation.

So the real challenge is an affective one. It is imperative that the teachers respond and own this aspect of the curriculum to the extent that they own their own consensus driven one. To do this, schools must not assume that since boilerplate curriculum is externally driven, it requires little or no internal attention. It does; it's just that the attention is of a different nature. To increase the possibility of creating the proper level of teacher ownership and responsiveness to boilerplate curriculum, take the following steps:

1. Determine how much of the boilerplate curriculum the teaching staff would have placed into the local curriculum through consensus if that opportunity had been present.
2. Then, for those learning objectives that would not have been consensus items, spend time on deciding how to teach them in such a way as to move them closer to the mission of the school, and thus hopefully create more ownership among the teachers.
3. Remember, what you do not do is more important than what you do. Don't be negative. Keep a positive attitude. Show that boilerplate is not the majority of the curriculum. It is the basic skill component, the foundation for the rest of the curriculum. Make it work for you.

Locally Required Curriculum

The locally required component of the curriculum program requires consensus. Because these learning objectives will be required for all students, and they will be a part of the formal assessment program, it will take significant time and effort to arrive at their identification. Along with the boilerplate mandates, this curriculum component represents the quality assessment items or the accountability piece. The school system should ensure that components of the quality triangle, consisting of the planned curriculum, instruction, and assessment, are correlated.

Elective Curriculum

Although consensus is not required, because the content is neither universal to all students nor a part of the formal assessment process, the elective curriculum is very important for any school that wants to meet the needs of its entire student body. In other words, if the school wishes to reach beyond required curriculum and maximize the opportunity for every student, regardless of ability, this component of the curriculum program is vital.

The learning objectives and outcomes of the elective curriculum should have both enrichment (horizontal) and acceleration (vertical) potential. Care must be taken to design an assessment component for this curriculum. Even though these learning objectives are not formally institutionally assessed, their achievement is vital to those students to whom they are relevant. Accountability is just as important in elective curriculum as it is in required curriculum.

SOURCES OF CURRICULUM

Reinhartz and Beach's interpretation of Tyler's[1] model for curriculum development suggests that the sources of curriculum are (1) the needs of the learners, (2) subject matter specialists, and (3) the values of society. Before a curriculum decision-making group begins determining scope and sequence for learning objectives, it should examine each of these three sources to ensure that the needs of each have been satisfied.

- Needs of learners: The discussion should begin with the needs of the learners. Are they typical for the subject content? If so, you could take the literature and research as the basic needs with a high degree of confidence. If not, identify the unique needs that must also be accommodated. These unique needs should not replace the universal needs but would, instead, be in addition to them. Finally, categorize the needs as cognitive, affective, and psychomotor. Then, during the curriculum development process, cross-check to make sure you have covered the needs of the learners by the categories.

- Subject matter specialists: The basic subject matter specialists for curriculum development are the teachers who will be implementing the curriculum design. As discussed in chapter 4, involvement in the development process is the most effective way to create and maintain the ownership and responsiveness necessary to ensure effective curriculum implementation. However, some questions need to be asked. Does the staff, by itself, constitute a complete and comprehensive team? Do they have the expertise to do the job? If not, what other subject matter specialists are needed? Identify them and decide how to get their input. The biggest challenge is to ensure that this group pays attention to the needs of the learners, outside subject matter specialists, and the values of the society they serve.
- Values of society: Correlating the values of society with the curriculum development will be a challenge if the society has significantly different values from those of the school's professional staff. Therefore, the participants in the curriculum development process should discuss what societal values could come into play during the development process. If you don't know them, you need a process to identify them. Most important, ask them in the context of curriculum, not general philosophical questions. This discussion also needs to take into consideration the political realities of the area that may impact upon the values reflected in the curriculum discussion.

Educational Screens for Curriculum Sources

Psychology of Learning

The psychology of learning is more important during the implementation phase of curriculum than the design phase because that's where student learning takes place. The psychology of learning is included in the discussion of philosophy in chapter 2. But it is also important in the design phase, because knowledge of the psychology of learning will guide the developers in knowing how many instructional objectives can reasonably fit into the planned curriculum, assist in determining the form of the objectives, and assist in determining the nature of the objectives.

Incorporating the Source and Screen into the Curriculum Development Process

Before beginning the actual curriculum process (working model and workshops), the participants should first, through consensus, answer the following questions:

- What are the needs of the learners?
- Who will be the subject matter specialists? Are the participants adequate? If not, what other subject matter specialists are needed, and how will they be accessed?

- What values of our society (community) should be a source of the objectives? Or, what values will affect the subject matter content and how?
- What principles of the psychology of learning must we incorporate in the objectives or their teaching?
- How will the process ensure that the educational philosophy of the school and the program philosophy permeate the instructional objectives?

Armed with this information, derived from a process emphasizing discussion and consensus, participants are now fully prepared to decide, by consensus, the specific instructional objectives that will make up the curriculum.

NOTE

1. Judy Reinhartz and Don M. Beach, *Secondary Education: Focus on Curriculum* (New York: HarperCollins, 1992), 150.

Chapter 6

Curriculum Documents

Good curriculum documents are the foundation of a successful curriculum program. The documents are not an end but the means to an end. They are the tangible evidence of the existence of curriculum. Therefore, the ongoing development and revision of quality curriculum documents should be a top priority for curriculum leaders.

TYPES OF CURRICULUM DOCUMENTS

Two types of documents are the most common products of curriculum development—the course of study and the curriculum resource guide. Some school systems combine these into one document; others separate them. Their functions are related but distinct.

- Course of study: The course of study prescribes what is to be taught in the classrooms of the school district. It is a working document that gives structure and direction to the educational program. The philosophy of the subject area, as stated in the course of study, should be consistent with the stated philosophy of the school system. Goals and objectives should be those that best meet the needs of that district's pupils. Evaluation policies should be those that permit an accurate assessment of the extent to which objectives are being met.
- Curriculum resource guide: A curriculum resource guide is suggestive in nature. Unlike the course of study, the resource guide does not prescribe scope and sequence. It is an instructional framework or aid designed to assist the teacher in implementing the course of study. Table 6.1 outlines the different functions of the course of study and the curriculum resource guide.

Table 6.1.   A Comparison of the Course of Study and Curriculum Resource Guide

Course of Study	Curriculum Resource Guide
1. Prescribes what is taught in a given subject or area of study.	1. Proposes how a subject or area of study may be taught.
2. Defines the educational program in terms of philosophy, goals, and learner objectives/outcomes.	2. Contains suggestions as to instructional framework, aids, materials, learning activities, teaching strategies, technology, and assessment items.
3. Is the official curriculum and thus can be changed only with the approval of the board of education or other official agency.	3. Is revised, altered, or amended at the discretion of school personnel.

Elements of a Quality Course of Study

1. Statement or Indication of Approval: The board of education (public schools) or an official agency must approve curriculum content.
2. Table of Contents
3. Introduction: An introduction should explain the purpose of the document and give a description or definition of its contents.
4. Program Philosophy
5. Scope and Sequence
6. Document Evaluation Policy: Describes who, what, when, and how the document will be evaluated

Elements of a Quality Curriculum Resource Guide

1. Correlation with the Course of Study: The purpose of the curriculum resource guide is to assist the teacher in effectively implementing the course of study. Therefore, every suggestion contained in the curriculum guide should be keyed to the course of study objective to which it applies.
2. Correlation with Teaching and Learning: A learning objective defines what should be taught, but in many cases it does not reflect what actually takes place in classrooms. Curriculum teams who define their beliefs about teaching and learning, and include best instructional practices in a curriculum resource guide, provide coherence between learning objectives and instruction.
3. Suggested Learning Activities: This section should be a combination of commercially prepared learning activities and those developed through the expertise of your own staff.
4. Correlation with Textbooks, Technology, and Materials Textbooks: Technology and instructional materials that are available to the teacher should be aligned with each learning objective in the course of study.

5. Criterion-Referenced Test Items: The curriculum must be accountable. The school must confirm how their students are doing on the school's planned curriculum. Standardized tests that are nationally normed may or may not be measuring the curriculum of the school. Criterion- or curriculum-referenced test items will measure the achievement of students in relation to the school's curriculum. The school that wants to verify how its students are doing in relation to the school's curriculum has only two ways to find out:

- Develop and administer criterion- or curriculum-referenced test items.
- Do an item analysis of the standardized test that you are using and check to see if your planned curriculum is being tested.

ALIGNING CURRICULUM WITH INSTRUCTION THROUGH RESOURCE GUIDES

Unfortunately, as previously noted, developing learning objectives does not always reflect the actual teaching and learning that occurs in classrooms. School districts, county schools, and independent schools have an opportunity to go beyond development of learning objectives and focus their attention on aligning instruction with the curriculum. Of course, suggested books, technology, software, websites, materials, common assessments, and so on can be included in the guide to provide additional, beneficial support for teachers. However, curriculum teams who stretch beyond resources and spend extended time researching and discussing best teaching practices cultivate teachers and strengthen instructional skills. Developing instructional frameworks and mapping the curriculum are two examples of formative, curriculum development processes.

An instructional framework is a powerful form of collaboration among teachers to effectively impact student learning. An instructional framework is a shared belief, philosophy, or understanding of a set of instructional principles, founded on research, which are implemented in the classrooms. Various forms of instructional frameworks have been developed to align with a school's instructional philosophy and tailored to meet the school's needs.

The curriculum work begins with the team examining research-based, professional practices to determine shared beliefs and to build common understandings of teaching and learning. The process can be tedious as teachers have different views of effective instruction, and a multitude of strategies exist. Over time, as the team's belief becomes solidified, the team analyzes data to understand if there is a connection between their belief system and actual classroom instructional practices.

The ultimate goal is to create an instructional framework of proven components, which assist teachers in implementing high quality teaching and learning. Some examples of instructional frameworks include higher order thinking, differentiation, integration of digital tools, and gradual release of responsibility.

Advantages to instructional frameworks include the following:

- A shared belief and approach to teaching and learning
- Vertical and horizontal discussions on and sharing of research-based instructional practices and strategies
- Exemplary models and approaches to teaching
- Quality lessons
- Improved teaching
- Powerful professional development

Curriculum mapping is another example of aligning the curriculum with instruction. Mapping is a process whereby teachers record or "map" on a chart or spreadsheet what subjects, topics, and skills were actually taught in the classroom, in what time frame, and in what order. The end result is a curriculum map, or working document, that reveals "what is being taught over the course of a year, within a unit of study, and even down to a specific lesson. Often, a map for a lesson will include essential questions, the content that will be covered, skills students will demonstrate if they understand the content, assessments, and activities" aligned to the learning objectives. Figure 6.1 illustrates a sample map template organized by months. Over time,

Curriculum Map Template

	August/ September	October	November	December
Standard(s)				
Essential Question(s)				
Content				
Skills/Understandings				

Figure 6.1. Map Organized by Month

other resources, instructional materials, and best-practice lesson plans can also be included to create a more comprehensive curriculum guide.

Advantages to curriculum mapping include the following:

- Analysis of what is being taught, when, and in what order
- Identification of gaps and repetition in instruction
- Alignment of curriculum, instruction, and assessment with the standards
- Collaboration within and across grade levels and content resulting in a vertical and horizontal view of curriculum and instruction
- Interdisciplinary connections
- Effective teaching strategies and resources shared

Schools and teachers are accountable for impacting student's academic growth from year to year. Developing an instructional framework or creating a curriculum map are meaningful professional development processes that not only provides a more comprehensive curriculum document to guide teachers but ultimately leads to implementation of best teaching practices and improved student achievement.

FORMAT AND CONTENT EVALUATION OF CURRICULUM DOCUMENTS

For a curriculum document to have quality, it must meet the needs and expectations of its users in both format and content. Obviously, if the content is weak, the document will be of little value. But even if the content is good, the document will still not be properly or adequately used if the format is weak. It is true that if the content is strong, then from a design perspective, the document is strong. However, from the delivery perspective, the document would still be weak because the format makes the document difficult to use. Therefore, in many instances, it would be used, or more likely not used, to its maximum strength. From the perspective of this book, curriculum documents are strong only if they can be maximized in both the curriculum design and instructional implementation functions. Hence equal attention and value are given to format and content.

The format evaluation should center on the criterion of usability. In technology terms, the document should be user-friendly. The content evaluation should be conducted from the perspective of how effective the document is as a management tool for curriculum.

Some schools combine the course of study and the curriculum resource guide into one document. Others separate them. Regardless of the design, all curriculum documents should be evaluated on format and content.

Format Evaluation

The format evaluation should assess the following elements of the document:

Online document
Introduction
Binding
Program philosophy
Numbering system
Scope and sequence
Articulation
Evaluation policy
Board of education approval
Lesson plan correlation
Table of contents

Online

A curriculum guide needs to be a fluid document. New research, materials, websites, assessments, mandated requirements, and so on are continually introduced and impact curriculum. By placing a curriculum guide online, the document can be edited effortlessly. Instructional resources, such as model lesson plans, instructional frameworks, and curriculum maps, can be added to the document as teachers implement the curriculum. So the guide is not a fixed document until the next revision process. It is adaptable, flexible, available to all stakeholders, and current.

Hard copy

An online document may be adaptable but may lack ease of use. Teachers may prefer a hard copy of the document, so they can write notes in the margins, attach activities, or easily flip to another section. Both online and hard copy documents should be made available.

Binding

The best bindings for a hard copy document are spiral bound or three-hole punched. These types of binding allow the document to lie flat when opened. When the teacher opens it to a certain page, the book lies flat and remains open and therefore easily readable without having to be held open with the hand or fingers. This may seem to be an insignificant consideration in evaluating a format. But it is not. Any time the teacher is using the curriculum document, either planning or actual instruction is occurring. In either case, the teacher needs both hands free.

Numbering System

The numbering system should allow for the addition and deletion of learning objectives without changing the numbers of the existing learning objectives. If the course of study stood alone, this would not be so vital. But other documents are correlated with the course of study. They are curriculum resource guides; competency, proficiency, and standardized tests; and individual student record-keeping systems that document the student's progress in curricular areas. If the number of an objective in the course of study is changed, then all the other documents must also be changed. Therefore, the numbering system should accommodate the revision process with the least amount of number changes possible. With the advent of technology systems that have lessened the reliance on hard copy documentation, the adherence to numbering systems has become less significant. Changing numbers or any other component can be easily achieved with advanced technology. However, if hard copy documentation is still being utilized, a number system that lends itself to the addition of learning objectives is still vital.

Based on these criteria, the following numbering system is recommended.

First objective #005
Second objective #010
Third objective #015
And so on

This numbering system would allow for four additional objectives to be added before the existing numbering system would have to be changed.

Based on these criteria, the following numbering system is not recommended.

First objective #1
Second objective #2
Third objective #3
And so on

This numbering system would mean that any additional objectives would have to carry numbers like 1a, 1b, 2a, 2b, and so on. As revisions continue, the numbers would have to carry three digits (e.g., 12a-2). Such numbering systems are cumbersome and hard to read.

Articulation

Previous and subsequent grade levels or subjects that are either prerequisites or postrequisites should be readily available to the teacher. A K–12 format is best. However, if such a wide span makes the document too cumbersome, then the document should at least contain plus or minus two grade levels, or the immediate prerequisite and postrequisite subject (assuming the subject has prerequisites or postrequisites).

Board of Education Approval

The document should contain a letter or statement that it has been approved by the appropriate governing body. A course of study is a legal document in most states and thus must be approved by officers of the school district. The date of the adoption should also be included.

Table of Contents

A curriculum document table of contents should be explicit, so that the teacher can find any curricular topic quickly. Many curriculum areas are very broad. If the table of contents lists only these broad curricular areas, it will be of little use. For example, communication skills could contain many different learning objectives. The table of contents should break down communication skills into its components so the teacher can quickly find the appropriate subject objectives.

Introduction

The introduction should explain all symbols used throughout the document. Learning objectives often contain additional designations. For example, proficiency items are marked with a P, career awareness objectives with a CA, required objectives with an R, and competency items with a C. Other possible designations could be italics for spiraled objectives and bold for standardized test items.

Program Philosophy

The program philosophy component should clearly spell out the vision, mission, and philosophical beliefs that will drive the curriculum implementation. The philosophy should be compatible with the school district philosophy.

Scope and Sequence

The learning objectives include a scope and sequence. However, the reader would have to read the entire document to comprehend its totality. A scope and sequence chart or matrix that shows when and where learning objectives are introduced, spiraled (reinforced), and assessed for mastery is helpful in seeing the total curriculum laid out in an abbreviated, yet comprehensive form.

Evaluation Policy

Curriculum documents have two different evaluation policies. First is the policy regarding how the organization develops and assesses the utility of the document. Second is the policy regarding how the students who are engaged in the learning experience are assessed.

- Organization: This policy should answer three questions: (a) Who was responsible for the development of the document? (b) How was the document developed? (process), and (c) When did the development occur and when will the revision take place?
- Student: This policy should tell how the students are going to be assessed and what level of performance is acceptable.

Lesson Plan Correlation

The purpose of curriculum documents is to facilitate instruction. Lesson plans are the formal means of transferring curriculum design into instruction. The course of study and the curriculum resource guide should make it easy for the teacher to prepare lesson plans. If the learning objectives are written cleanly, concisely, and measurably, the teacher can simply write in the numbers of the objectives that are being covered in the planned lesson. This would take only a few seconds or minutes. Then the teacher has more time to think about the most important thing: how do I teach this lesson well?

Needless to say, the lesson plan format must lend itself to this correlation. The lesson plan format should contain spaces for inserting the learning objective numbers from the course of study that will be taught in the lesson. The lesson plan book should indicate that anyone wishing to know the content of the numbered objectives should consult the course of study.

Instrument for Evaluating Curriculum Document Format

Next is an example of an instrument that evaluates curriculum document hard copy format. See figure 6.2.

Content Evaluation

The content evaluation should be based on five criteria:

1. Clarity and validity of learning objectives
2. Correlation between the curriculum design and the testing/evaluation process

3. Delineation by prerequisites of the essential skills, knowledge, and attitudes
4. Delineation of major instructional tools
5. Clear linkages for classroom utilization

The first three criteria pertain to the course of study. The fourth and fifth criteria refer to the curriculum resource guide.

Clarity and Validity of Learning Objectives

This criterion is listed first because it is the most basic of all the content components. Learning objectives make up at least 80 percent of the total curriculum document. In addition, the other four criteria are either based on the learning objectives or dependent upon them for their nature and existence.

Clear and valid learning objectives will contain the following elements:

• States tasks to be performed or skills to be learned.
• States what, when, and how the actual standard of measurement is performed—the time required to teach the learning objectives is equal to the time prescribed for the teaching of the learning objectives. In other words, the course of study should not contain so many learning objectives that the teacher cannot possibly cover the course content in the time allotted.

One of the biggest weaknesses of many curriculum documents is that not enough consideration has been given to the function of time in the learning process. The adult world is full of people who have never studied any American history beyond 1960. There is simply too much content in American history to teach it all. Therefore, too many curriculums were designed chronologically and comprehensively; as a result, the school year ended without the teacher being able to teach the most recent eras. This problem must be dealt with during the design phase of curriculum development. When establishing the validity and clarity of learning objectives, part of that decision must be based on the time allotted to the course or subject. Needless to say, this decision will often be based on abandonment or prioritization.

Correlation between Curriculum Design and the Testing/ Evaluation Process

If curriculum documents are going to be the tools of curriculum management, then the correlation between the design and testing/evaluation process must be a "tight" fit. Generalities and assumptions won't do. Two components must be present for this correlation to have congruity. First, the skills,

Hard Copy Format Design		
(Descriptors)	Unacceptable	Acceptable
1. Online *Document is posted online in adaptable format*	0 1 2	3 4 5
2. Binding *Document lies flat when opened; i.e. uses spiral or 3-hole binding*	0 1 2	3 4 5
3. Numbering System *Allows for the additional of goals, objectives, and outcomes without changing numbers of the existing ones.*	0 1 2	3 4 5
4. Articulation *At least two previous and subsequent grade levels or prerequisite courses are readily available to the teacher.*	0 1 2	3 4 5
5. Board of Education Approval *Letter should include date of board approval*	0 1 2	3 4 5
6. Table of Contents *Has sufficient specificity and clarity to allow teacher to quickly find the desired content*	0 1 2	3 4 5
7. Introduction *Explains all symbols used in the document that are not self-explanatory.*	0 1 2	3 4 5
8. Program Philosophy *Is understandable; correlates with school philosophy, vision, and mission.*	0 1 2	3 4 5
9. Scope and Sequence *Clearly delineates when learning objectives are introduced, reinforced, and assessed.*	0 1 2	3 4 5
10. Organization Review of Document *Tells how students will be assessed on the learning objectives and the acceptable level of performance.*	0 1 2	3 4 5
11. Student Evaluation Policy *Tells how students will assessed on the learning objectives and the acceptable level of performance.*	0 1 2	3 4 5
12. Lesson Plan Correlation *How well is the lesson plan format and content correlated with the course of study and curriculum resource guide? Does it facilitate the writing of lesson plans?*	0 1 2	3 4 5

Figure 6.2.   Curriculum Document Format Evaluation Instrument

knowledge, and concepts to be assessed are explained. Then the learning objectives representing these skills, knowledge, and concepts are keyed to the performance evaluation (criterion- or curriculum-referenced tests) and to the district tests (norm-referenced) in use.

Delineation by Prerequisites of the Essential Skills, Knowledge, and Attitudes

This delineation will vary according to the organizational structure of the school. For example, the delineation could be by grade in the graded structure or by student achievement level in the nongraded structure. Regardless of the organizational structure, the curriculum document should include all specific prerequisite skills or knowledge required for the learning experience. Any prior needed experience for the grade level or the course should be listed.

Two additional criteria are found in curriculum resource guides if the resource guide is bound separately from the course of study. These are Delineation of Major Instructional Tools and Clear Linkages for Classroom Utilization. Some schools choose to bind the course of study and the resource guide in one document.

Delineation of Major Instructional Tools

This criterion specifies the textbooks, technology, and learning materials used to teach the learning objectives. To be an excellent criterion, it must not only contain a list of all textbooks, technology, and supplementary materials to be

Curriculum Document Content	Date of Review	Reviewer
(Descriptors)	*Unacceptable*	*Acceptable*
Clarity and Validity of Learning Objectives *States tasks to be performed or skills to be learned, and what, when, how actual standard of measurement is performed. Also, objectives match time allotted for the learning experience.)*	0 1 2	3 4 5
Correlation between the Curriculum Design and the Testing/Evaluation Process *Skills, knowledge, and concepts that will be assessed are explained and objectives are keyed to performance evaluation and district tests, criterion- and norm-referenced, in use*	0 1 2	3 4 5
Delineation by Prerequisites of the Essential Skills, Knowledge, and Attitudes Prior experiences needed, specific prerequisites documented, or description of discrete skills required.)	0 1 2	3 4 5
Delineation of Major Instructional Tools *Basic textbooks and supplementary materials included, and a "match" between the textbooks/ materials and the curriculum objective by objective..*	0 1 2	3 4 5
Clear Linkages for Classroom Utilization *Specific examples on how to approach key concepts and skills in the classroom*	0 1 2	3 4 5

Figure 6.3.   Curriculum Document Content Evaluation Instrument

used but also indicate a "match"—objective by objective—between the list and the curriculum document.

Clear Linkages for Classroom Utilization

The key to this criterion is the inclusion of specific examples on how to approach the most significant concepts and skills in the classroom. Most certainly, all proficiencies, competencies, and any other objectives assessed in the testing program would be included.

Figure 6.3 is an example of an instrument that can be used to evaluate curriculum document content.

Chapter 7

Curriculum Program Evaluation

ELEMENTS OF SUMMATIVE CURRICULUM EVALUATION

In evaluating the curriculum program, the school system should examine the following elements that affect the quality of the curriculum program.[1]

To use only one element will not provide a comprehensive evaluation of the total dynamics of curriculum.

Evaluation Element 1: Objectives/Outcomes

Element I evaluates how students are doing on objectives/outcomes based on testing and assessment measures.

A. Examples

1. Proficiency tests
2. Competency-based education
3. Skills-based programs

B. Assumptions

1. Learner outcomes are the best measure of curriculum.
2. The stated objectives/outcomes are the true intent of the curriculum.
3. Particular outcomes are significant for all learners.
4. There is congruence between the curriculum outcomes and student achievement.
5. How students are taught (means) is not as important as how they perform on the objectives/outcomes (ends).

C. Positive Forces for Use

    1. It is widely used because it is the only universal, politically acceptable element of curriculum evaluation.
    2. It focuses the curriculum effort among staff.
    3. It is quantitative in nature, thus producing effect of objectivity.

D. Negative Forces for Use

    1. Focus is narrow.
    2. It ignores or does not explain program dynamics such as individual differences among learners, psychology of learning, learning styles, and diverse or alternative assessment measures.

E. Why It Should Be an Element of Curriculum Evaluation

    1. Measures core or basic curriculum
    2. Answers the call for accountability from the body politic
    3. Identifies differences between curriculum design and implementation

Evaluation Element 2: Decision Making

Element 2 evaluates the decision-making structure of the school. This evaluation element places a high priority on leadership and management as vital to the success of a curriculum program. It is a systems approach to evaluating curriculum based on intended and actual means and intended and actual ends.

A. Examples

    1. All systems approaches to curriculum development revolving around intended means, actual means, intended ends, and actual ends[2]

B. Assumptions

    1. Curriculum decision making is rational and logical.
    2. If an effective decision-making structure is in place, it will produce an effective curriculum.

C. Positive Forces for Use

    1. It is a continuous improvement process.
    2. Incorporates school leadership as a prerequisite for quality curriculum, thus increasing administrative involvement and placing teachers in leadership roles.

D. Negative Forces for Use

    1. Decision making is often political.
    2. It requires continual gathering of information on a timely basis.
    3. It requires ongoing, continuous evaluation, which tends to lessen support.

E. Why It Should Be an Element of Curriculum Evaluation

    1. It provides the curriculum program with strategic and long-term planning.

Evaluation Element 3: Organizational Development

Element 3 is consistent with the human relations approach to organizational management built on the continuous improvement theorists such as Deming, Sholtes, Juran, Glasser, Senge, and others. The element assesses the dynamic energy and renewal that comes from ongoing organizational development. This element is at the heart of the learning organization.

A. Examples

    1. Professional growth opportunities for staff and leaders
    2. Problem solving in curriculum and staff development
    3. Human relations and communications activities

B. Assumptions

    1. Open communications can be helpful in solving conflicts.
    2. Diverse positions, including bias, must be aired to allow growth.

C. Positive Forces for Use

    1. Improves staff problem-solving skills
    2. Increases staff involvement in curriculum issues

D. Negative Forces for Use

    1. Human conflict and discussion lead attention away from basic curriculum issues.
    2. This element may need outside consultant to maintain focus on issues.
    3. It creates need for advocacy of data as a driving force for curriculum content.

E. Why It Should Be an Element of Curriculum Evaluation

    1. Increases staff input and involvement, thus combating faculty burnout and apathy
    2. Provides a process to resolve staff conflict and tension
    3. Opens up closed communications
    4. Is vital to innovative curriculum projects

Evaluation Element 4: External Judgment

One of Deming's[3] principles is that profound knowledge comes from outside the organization. Kuhn[4] supports this notion in his research on paradigms with the claim that new rules and regulations, and thus new paradigms, usually come from the "fringes," or from people not vested in the current paradigm. This element brings external expertise to curriculum evaluation.

A. Examples

    1. School self-study
    2. Accreditation boards review (North Central, etc.)
    3. External evaluation (audit, feasibility study, etc.)

B. Assumptions

    1. Expertise is an excellent method of evaluating curriculum.
    2. Consensus from a status group is valid.
    3. Program evaluation is stronger if it includes both an internal and external component.

C. Positive Forces for Use

    1. Expertise can be used to solve problems.
    2. Recommendations can be made in a timely fashion.
    3. It provides a political base for decision making.

D. Negative Forces for Use

    1. Experts and status persons may be unable to grasp the essence of local cultural issues that affect the curriculum.
    2. Experts and status persons may not have the time to thoroughly evaluate the school's curriculum.

E. Why It Should Be an Element of Curriculum Evaluation

    1. External judgment carries great political influence.
    2. When curriculum change is planned that will affect the community (e.g., sex education, controversial social topics, curriculum on which diversity is acute), judgment evaluation will give the school the data and information it needs to make curriculum decisions.
    3. Internal self-studies are enhanced by the process of having to explain and defend the curriculum to non-stakeholders and neutral examiners.

Evaluation Element 5: Research

Element 5 is based on the scientific method. It involves forming hypotheses, isolating variables, and determining such issues as variance and significant differences. It is the least-used element of evaluation at the school level because of societal resistance to educational experiments that involve the students. As one parent put it, "Research all you want, but don't experiment with my kid." There is great potential to the increased use of this element. Using research as a basis for curriculum change could lessen schools' tendency to participate in fads that have little lasting effect on teaching and learning.

A. Examples

1. Goal-free evaluation studies
2. Examining critical variables using scientific research techniques
3. Validating learner performance based on curriculum (standardized or criterion-referenced)
4. Instructional research

B. Assumptions

1. It is possible to isolate critical variables in curriculum and instruction.
2. Pure research can be performed without endangering the learning of individual students.

C. Positive Forces for Use

1. It minimizes bias because it is goal-free.
2. It is a vigorous approach to curriculum evaluation.

D. Negative Forces for Use

1. It is time consuming.
2. Halo effect of a test can achieve more than one critical variable.
3. It is difficult to do in school setting without interfering with the instructional program.

E. Why It Should Be an Element of Curriculum Evaluation

1. New curriculum designs should include research and development.

FORMATIVE CURRICULUM EVALUATION

Summative curriculum evaluation occurs at the end of a cycle and is designed to formulate a judgment about the quality of the curriculum being evaluated and to make decisions based on that summative judgment. These decisions could range from discontinuing the curriculum to making revisions within its current structure.

Continuous Improvement Processes

Formative curriculum evaluation is ongoing. Its purpose is continuous improvement. The continuous improvement standard is based on the assumption that regardless of the current success of the current curriculum, there is always the opportunity to improve. Formative evaluation is not designed to identify deficiencies or major problems. The process is designed to continuously improve. Sometimes the motivation is based on trying to solve a problem. However, at other times the process is not based on any deficiency, only the desire to do better.

To effectively use continuous improvement, the organization must know how to benchmark. Benchmarking is the process of gathering reliable data and information to accurately assess your current performance. Then, after you have properly benchmarked your current performance, quality improvement tools are used to move toward higher levels of performance.

Formative evaluation through continuous improvement does not use numerical goals. Numerical goals are a part of summative evaluation processes. Continuous improvement uses benchmarks (current performance) and works toward the betterment of performance.

Continuous Improvement Tools

Here are some processes that formative curriculum evaluation should seek to address by gathering data, benchmarking, and taking collective action through the use of quality improvement tools and the technology mind-set.

- Obtaining ongoing teacher feedback about the quality of curriculum design, instruction, and compatibility of the two functions
- Assessing effectiveness of the curriculum development process
- Clarifying the system's curriculum implementation (instruction) processes or problems
- Determining whether the curriculum/instructional program is a stable system
- Analyzing student achievement data
- Analyzing the school system's capacity to change

Curriculum Process	Improvement Tools
Teacher Feedback	Affinity/Relations/Systemic Diagrams
Curriculum Development	Flow Charts
Systems Processes/Problems	Operational Definitions/Cause and Effect Charts
Stable Systems	Control Charts
Student Achievement	Control Charts/Bar Charts
Curriculum Change	Force Field Analysis
Relationships	Scatter Chart/Relations Chart
Categorizing Problems	Pareto Chart

Figure 7.1.   Example of Quality Improvement Tool for Curriculum Processes

- Determining the relationship between two factors that are affecting curriculum effectiveness
- Separating the "vital few" problems from the "trivial many"

Figure 7.1 presents a quality improvement tool that could be used to work toward continuous improvement in the curriculum processes just listed.

NOTES

1. John C. Hill, *Curriculum Evaluation for School Improvement* (Springfield, IL: Charles C. Thomas, 1986), 66.

2. D. L. Stufflebean and A. J. Shinkfield, *Systematic Evaluation* (Boston: Kluwe-Nijhoff, 1985).

3. W. Edwards Deming, *The New Economics* (Cambridge: Massachusetts Institute of Technology, 1993), 94.

4. Thomas H. Kuhn, *The Structure of Scientific Revolutions* (Chicago: University of Chicago Press, 1962).

REFERENCES

Glasser, William. (1990). *The quality school.* New York: Harper & Row.

Jenkins, Lee. (1997). *Improving student learning, applying Deming's quality principles in classrooms.* Milwaukee, WI: ASQ Quality Press.

Scholtes, Peter R. (1989). *The team handbook.* Madison, WI: Joiner Associates.

Senge, Peter M. (1990). *The fifth discipline: The art & practice of the learning organization.* New York: Doubleday.

Chapter 8

The Role of Paradigms
in Curriculum Change

Paradigms are models or patterns of thinking and behaving. They create the rules and regulations and establish the standards that define success within a field.[1] Problems are solved within the boundaries of these paradigms. However, paradigms often keep people from accepting new ideas.

There is a tendency for people to adjust data and information by filtering it through scientific mind-sets that agree with their paradigms. Therefore, data or information that agrees with their current paradigms are more likely to gain acceptance than data that disagree with the current paradigm. This is called the paradigm effect,[2] and it may blind people and organizations to new opportunities. It causes them to try to discover the future through the current paradigm. This, of course, limits people's thinking.

CURRENT PARADIGM IN PLANNED
CURRICULUM CHANGE

The current paradigm holds that planned curriculum change should be based on the following premise: verification of an existing deficiency.

Verification of an existing deficiency is a negative premise. However, it is a legitimate reason to alter an existing practice and move toward change designed to correct this deficiency. The verification of the deficiency is a necessary part of this premise. If the deficiency is verified, the support of the change to correct the deficiency will be better.

Chapter 8

NEW PARADIGM FOR PLANNED
CURRICULUM CHANGE

The new paradigm holds that planned curriculum change should also be based on the following two principles:

- The school will meet and exceed the needs and expectations of the key players and stakeholders of the school in planned curriculum change.
- Planned curriculum change will be based on the pursuit of continuous quality improvement as well as perceived or real deficiencies.

Meeting and Exceeding the Needs and Expectations of Key Players and Stakeholders

This operational definition, derived from the Total Quality literature,[3] means that the school will take a systems approach to planned curriculum change. The systems approach means that the school considers its key players and stakeholders as part of the system and that, therefore, they should be involved in the decisions concerning curriculum change.

This definition naturally raises the question: Who are the school's key players and stakeholders? The school has four key players, two primary and two secondary. The primary key players are the students and the parents. Secondary key players are institutions of continuing education and the students' future employers. Additional stakeholders in the school are all those people or organizations whose operation is directly or indirectly affected by the quality of school.

Critics of this operational definition of quality say that curriculum is a professional process that should be determined by educators. These critics believe that professional educators, who are knowledgeable and experienced in curriculum, should not have to listen to the opinions of the uninformed people.

First of all, in the public schools, the public, through its board of education, is in fact the final decision maker. So, the question is not whether the professional educators want the public to have input but how the professional curriculum worker is going to solicit and use the input. When dealing with tradition and other obstacles to planned change, it is preferable to have input and throughput from the key players and stakeholders during the process, as opposed to reaction to the output after the completion of the process.

Educators also need to pay close attention to the second part of the definition of quality: exceeding the key players' needs and expectations. It is in the exceeding of client needs and expectations that professional educators can provide their special expertise and experience. Remember, no client ever asked for differentiation, project-based learning, collaboration, blended learning, multiple intelligence approaches, or any of the other educational innovations that have had such a positive impact on students and schools. But they were more than glad to avail themselves of the benefits of these changes. Just because school communities have definite ideas about what should go on in their schools—and most do—does not mean that they won't listen to their professional educators. They always have, and given good reason, they always will.

So this definition of quality curriculum allows for a decision-making partnership with the key players and stakeholders of the school while simultaneously providing the avenue for professional curriculum leadership.

Continuous Improvement as the Standard for Planned Curriculum Change

Curriculum leaders using continuous improvement as the standard measure of success will have to be paradigm pioneers. Barker[4] refers to curriculum pioneers as people willing to innovate more on faith than on data. Remember, the definition of the paradigm includes the notion that the paradigm not only establishes the boundaries of the model but also establishes the rules for success. The current paradigm on curriculum change uses traditional scientific management principles to evaluate curriculum change. Specifically, the current standards for curriculum change are based on the following principles.

Numerical Goals

The deficiencies that currently determine most planned curriculum change are based on quantitative data, which prove that certain numerical goals are not being met. For example, if the standardized tests suggest that the students are not achieving well in math, but are achieving better in language arts, this data is used to determine that drastic changes are needed in math curriculum but not in language arts. The data might also cause a school system to alter their curriculum revision schedule, placing math as the top priority in time and resources.

Conversely, if the standardized test scores were high, the school system might decide not to revise or alter their curriculum in any way. Thus they are saying that, based on numerical goals, they have been successful. They will dispense with curriculum change until the data reveals that a deficiency has surfaced.

Written Curriculum——————— instruction————Supervision (Evaluation)

(Administrative function   (Teacher function)   (Administrative function)
with teacher input)

Figure 8.1. Pipeline Model

Curriculum Change Dependent on Supervision for Monitoring Improvement

Curriculum change has evolved within the larger movement to make schools "teacher-proof." By this I mean that the school continues to organize and operate in a manner that says "someone has to make sure these teachers are doing their jobs." In curriculum this means that safeguards are in place to protect the school from incompetent teaching. Primary among these safeguards are lesson plan procedures, very specific curriculum guidelines, and uniform testing programs.

To various degrees, teachers participate in writing the curriculum. That limited trust does not carry over into the curriculum delivery and evaluation processes. This infers that although teachers are capable of helping to determine the scope and sequence of curriculum, someone else must supervise the delivery system. Under this system teacher cannot change the curriculum when the need for improvement arises but must wait for a formal process at a later date. The process is shown in figure 8.1.

This is a pipeline model, which is a linear process. The functions are separated and run consecutively, not simultaneously. There is no freedom to change the system, which is imposed from above. Planned curriculum change can occur only after the evaluation process has been completed.

In most school systems, this pipeline model may take five years. So, in essence, if the curriculum needs change, students have gone through five years of inferior education waiting for the needed change to be planned and implemented.

USING CONTINUOUS IMPROVEMENT IN PLANNED CURRICULUM CHANGE

Continuous improvement in planned curriculum change is accomplished by discarding the pipeline model and replacing it with the cyclical model shown in figure 8.2.

This model views curriculum design, implementation, and evaluation as an ongoing cycle. Regarding curriculum quality control, the cycle shows that the three steps are not independent. Instead, they are interlocking. Designing

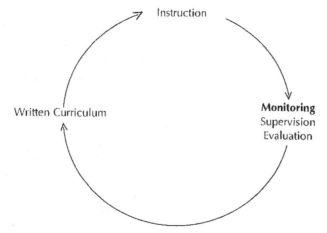

Figure 8.2.   Cyclical Model for Planned Curriculum Improvement

meaningful curriculum requires knowledge of how this curriculum design is delivered. Also, the evaluation must be based on both the curriculum design and the delivery.

In essence, the cyclical model approach to curriculum design creates a flexible system that is formulated in part by the people who use it, namely, the teachers. This flexibility allows teachers to respond to changes in the learning environment when they occur. There is less emphasis on forecasting, and greater emphasis on making the curriculum design work. This naturally leads to the concept of continual improvement.

As long as the curriculum design (and the document it produces) is viewed as being optimal, there is no freedom to alter the design. Under the pipeline model, there can be no improvement until it is time to revise the document. Obviously, when the design comes up for revision, the optimal status, which the curriculum design has enjoyed during its tenure, is temporarily removed until the new revision is completed. Then, optimal status is restored until the next revision cycle.

Under the pipeline model, continuous improvement is not an option. However, when teachers are no longer trapped within the curriculum design and development cycle imposed from above, they can begin to make needed changes in the system on an ongoing basis. Barriers to quality teaching due to poor curriculum design can be addressed immediately, not just at the end of the revision cycle. And perhaps most important, the teachers can begin to take more pride in their jobs; this type of continuous improvement allows teachers to contribute to their job in more ways than just teaching in their classroom. They can also contribute to the continual improvement of the curriculum.

The cyclical model infers that what curriculum change process needs in order to be successful is a professional teacher approach. The model places curriculum decision making in the hands of the teachers as well as the administrator or supervisor. It gives the teachers a legitimate and recognized role in both curriculum design and delivery. In fact, it tends to merge the two processes.

The idea of curriculum change being an ongoing process as opposed to an every-five-year review cycle (pipeline model) stops the practice of having teachers participate in curriculum design and then not having the power to make adjustments during the delivery phase. Such a paradigm shift as this would create a change in the natural work function of teachers. No longer would they be asked to separate the functions of curriculum design and delivery. During curriculum delivery, they would have the increased function of making continuous improvement in curriculum design.

The major reason that curriculum improvements have been slow in coming is that they are being pursued without a commensurate change in the natural work function of teachers. The most significant change that could occur in curriculum design and delivery is that of changing the natural work function of the people involved. In fact, changing the natural work function of teachers is the prerequisite for significant planned change in curriculum design and delivery.

The Importance of Teacher Natural Work Function to Planned Curriculum Change

To understand how teachers' natural work function affects planned curriculum change, it is first necessary to examine current teacher natural work function in curriculum design and delivery. Basically, teachers are participating in three curriculum functions: (1) writing curriculum, (2) implementing curriculum (instruction), and (3) monitoring (supervision) curriculum and the resulting evaluation.

- Writing the curriculum: Teachers are usually expected to perform this function in a series of from two to six workshops scheduled within a short time span (usually either one semester or a school year). These scheduled workshops usually last approximately six hours each. Sometimes they are held during school days with substitute teachers provided. Sometimes they are held after school, and sometimes on weekends, usually Saturday. Most significant is that teachers perform the function without being released from any of their teaching responsibilities.
- Implementing the curriculum (instruction): This is the current natural work function of teachers. In the day-to-day work of a teacher, this function makes up 95 to 99 percent of the workday. Using the pipeline model (see

figure 8.1), this is the only one of the three functions in which teachers are extensively involved. The assumption has always been that curriculum delivery is the only function that teachers need to be extensively involved in. The second assumption is that teachers can do a good job in this function without extensive involvement in the other two curriculum functions. Keep in mind that we are talking about the teachers' function in relation to the curriculum. Therefore, the functions being discussed relate to the organizational goals of curriculum articulation and coordination as opposed to the individual classroom performance of each teacher.

- Monitoring the curriculum (supervision and evaluation): Currently, in most schools, this is totally an administrative function. In some instances, the administration gives the teacher an advise-and-consent role. The same administration that decides to give the teachers this role can also take it away. It is not a part of the teacher's natural work function.

In conclusion, the current natural work function of teachers is that they implement planned change. However, they do not plan it, monitor it for success or failure, nor evaluate it to determine its future. The administration is responsible for these three teachers' functions. The level of teacher input is determined by the administration. Sometimes they choose to do the evaluations themselves. In most school systems, the administration has the responsibility to perform these functions as they see fit.

In essence, if schools wish to increase teacher involvement in planned curriculum change, the responsibilities of teachers will increase by two-thirds. This estimate is based on simple mathematical ratios. There are three functions; teachers are currently responsible for one. If they become involved in two additional functions, that will increase their responsibility by two-thirds. Since most teachers are in the classroom six hours out of seven during the school day, such an increase in job responsibilities without a change in natural work function is unthinkable. So the message is clear: teachers cannot assume a significant role in planned curriculum change unless there is a change in their natural work function.

Why Should Schools Change Teachers' Natural Work Functions?

Schools should contemplate changing teachers' natural work functions so that they can assist in planning curriculum changes, for the following reasons.

Improving Curriculum Design and Delivery

When the pipeline model is not producing improvement in curriculum design and delivery, change may be required. Most educational change is doing nothing more than "tinkering" with the system. No substantive planned change is taking place because schools cannot get the change to "take" at the operations level, the classroom. That is because teachers are not totally immersed in the planned change. They are totally involved only at the implementation level. Unfortunately, even that function is inadequate because the teachers aren't adequately involved in the functions of planning and monitoring. Since schools, as organizations, have not been successful in finding quality time for teachers to be involved in curriculum planning and monitoring, reform efforts and other planned changes have been attempted using the pipeline model. But it isn't working because teachers and other key operatives are only peripherally involved. Reforms have not been systemic changes, only procedural. The current system is that administration plans, teachers implement, and administration monitors and evaluates. Any systemic reform will have to alter this formula. To attempt planned change without changing this formula is to tinker with a stable system. Granted, the system is stable, but it is not successful. Therefore, the only way to improve it is to change it. The only way the system can be improved is to change the natural work function of teachers.

There are educational experts who wish to change teachers' natural work function by eliminating all their roles except teaching. Even though we oppose such a move because it would tend to move schools more toward the factory, quality control model, we find it preferable to the tinkering type of reform that asks more of teachers but does nothing to change their natural work function. However, the direction being proposed here is to move teachers' natural work function toward a more professional functioning, which includes playing a major role in all curriculum processes.

Giving the Cyclical Model a Chance to Succeed

The cyclical model being proposed would produce systemic change, provided it is accompanied by a shift in the natural work function of teachers. People and resources must be moved to the classroom level for the cyclical model to have a chance for success.

There is a great deal of evidence in other organizations that this shift from quality control to quality systems will produce better results in schools. The principle of placing the responsibility for quality at the operations level is the way American business and industry, both service and manufacturing, have been able to improve their position in the global economy. In fact, it is how the decay of America's competitiveness with Europe and Asia was checked.[5] So the notion of changing the natural work function of teachers is not based on an isolated hunch. It has worked in American business and industry. It is the basis of most quality systems in the world of work.

Getting More Input from Teachers

Teachers are the most knowledgeable organizational persons in curriculum delivery. They are the people closest to the process. They see on a daily basis what happens when curriculum design reaches the delivery function. This information is needed to plan curriculum design changes. Teachers currently have the knowledge. What they don't have is the time or the resources to perform the task. Teachers can obtain the needed time and resources only through a change in their natural work function.

Making the Cyclical Model Curriculum Design and Implementation Work

The cyclical model of curriculum design and implementation can succeed when schools use the following process:

1. Provide teacher training in teaming and decision making. These are the two functions that make up the planning, monitoring, and evaluation phases of planned curriculum change.
2. Provide quality time for the planning and the monitoring phases.
3. Make teacher performance assessment reflect the change in the natural work function of teachers to include planning, monitoring, and evaluation of curriculum.

Strategies for Systemically Changing Teachers' Natural Work Functions

Specific strategies will vary from school to school. Some school districts could immediately affect a change in natural work function. They already have the resources; they only lack the will. Other districts will have to undergo a change of priorities through a massive reallocation of resources. These reallocations will involve

- Increasing the number of classroom teachers at all levels to allow time for teacher involvement in curriculum planning, monitoring, and evaluation without hurting the quality of the instructional program.
- Bringing teaching out of isolation, so that quality instruction will take place when a teacher is absent from the classroom. This means changing from isolated, self-contained classrooms to cooperative, team-teaching organizational structures that free teachers from their natural work function without damaging instruction.
- Establishing the idea that professional learning must be a lifelong pursuit of teachers. It begins with strong induction programs for new teachers but extends even farther. "Induction is a highly organized and comprehensive

form of staff development, involving many people and components, that typically continues as a sustained process for the first two or five years of a teacher's career. Mentoring is often a component of the induction process . . . [but it] goes beyond the imparting of mere survival skills."[6]

- Reducing personnel in supervision and applying that money for classroom teaching units. If monitoring and evaluation become a teacher work function, there will be less need for curriculum supervisors.
- Recruiting, training, and utilizing a sophisticated teacher aide program, which increases the instructional staff and provides the flexibility needed for the shift in teacher natural work function.
- Giving curriculum a higher priority in budgeting than it currently receives. Do not treat curriculum as a function that can occur without funding. Even more vital is the assurance that money allocated for curriculum will not be used for non instructional emergencies.
- Adopting the practice of offering staff development programs that include professional growth in curriculum design and delivery.

It is interesting to note that most current planned curriculum change includes a prerequisite provision that the teaching staff must be supportive. It is a recognition that planned curriculum change cannot succeed without teacher support. That assumption is true, but it does not go far enough. It assumes the only commitment that curriculum change needs from the teachers is philosophical and attitudinal support. That is an incorrect assumption because, even if the teachers want the change to succeed, they do not have the time or the resources to make it happen. While the curriculum change process is in motion, they only have time to teach. The planned change becomes a secondary concern, perhaps even a distraction because it interferes with their natural work function and makes their job harder.

It is not difficult to understand why school reform seems to focus on school functions other than curriculum. In other administrative areas such as business practices, leadership theory, transportation, pupil personnel, and staff personnel, the teacher is not the only key player. Therefore, the planned change can be pursued without the necessity of a shift in teacher natural work function. But in planned curriculum change, the teacher is the key player. In fact, everyone else is just window dressing when compared to the teacher. Until the teachers' natural work function reflects this fact, planned curriculum change will continue to be less than true systemic change.

THE PLAN-DO-STUDY-ACT CYCLE

Once the natural work function of teachers has been changed so that the cyclical model of curriculum design and development can be followed, schools can begin to implement curriculum and instruction by using the Plan-Do-Study-Act (PDSA) cycle. The PDSA cycle (figure 8.3) looks like this:

This PDSA cycle addresses not only the internal feedback for curriculum design and delivery improvement but also the external feedback for adapting to, and even anticipating, curriculum trends. When these feedback types are combined, the benefit and strength of the cyclical model is apparent.

The cyclical nature of PDSA matches the way people learn and contribute to the world around them. When teachers are made a part of the natural operation, they facilitate incremental improvements. Because incremental improvements are easier to implement than major breakthroughs, the school becomes more responsive, more flexible. New content, technologies, and methodologies are more easily adopted, and curriculum delivery problems can be fixed in successive cycles as the curriculum design and delivery processes are continually refined.

Using continuous improvement in the curriculum development process changes the nature of goal setting. In the traditional process (the pipeline model-curriculum, instruction, and evaluation), the curriculum design or finished document will represent the goals of the curriculum design, or the finished document will represent the goals of the curriculum. The cyclical model, on the other hand, will replace these arbitrary goals with benchmarking. These benchmarks are based on monitoring actual student performance.

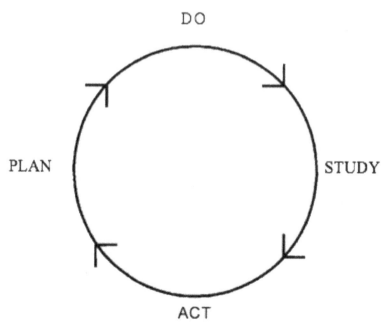

Figure 8.3. The PDSA Cycle

Therefore, the benchmarks can be used to continually improve both the curriculum design and the curriculum delivery.

The use of the continuous improvement standard puts the process of curriculum largely into the hands of the teachers. That is because they are the only people who work with both the curriculum design and delivery on a daily basis. This standard reflects the theory that quality is best achieved by placing the ultimate responsibility for quality at the operations level.

Currently, in many states, statutes outlining the governance of school curriculum would present obstacles to continuous improvement utilizing the cyclical PDSA process. For example, many states require that all courses of study be officially approved by both the local board of education and the state education authority. Therefore, the school utilizing continuous improvement in curriculum design and delivery will have to implement continuous improvement at the level allowed by the law. For example, if the state requires approval of all educational outcomes, then the school could work in continuous improvement only within the context of those outcomes. If the state requires approval of all goals, then the school could work with continuous improvement in the objectives used to achieve these goals.

This is not that big a constraint, because it is at the pupil performance level that learning is taking place anyway. So long as the school has the flexibility to work with the operations level (pupil performance objectives), the continuous improvement process for curriculum design and delivery is feasible.

The PDSA cycle suggests that curriculum change should be based on data, not hunches or even national trends or opinion. This data should come from the current performance within the school. This is not to suggest that national trends based on research should be ignored. However, if local data suggest that the national trend being considered is not "right" for the local situation, the local data should take precedence. By approaching planned change in this manner, schools can avoid the problem of following trends and fads and instead can implement those curriculum changes that are needed based on data from the educational setting.

It has long been held within the educational community that beyond basic skills, a national curriculum is not feasible due to the diversity of communities and differences of opinion on the primary mission of schools. Following the PDSA cycle will enable a school system to maintain its local autonomy while reacting to genuine need for curriculum change.

The PDSA cycle perceives planned curriculum change as a long-term, ongoing series of small steps as opposed to one gigantic step occurring periodically. Here is what each step in the PDSA cycle should entail:

- Plan: This phase is based on the best current thinking, knowledge, data, and information. It should include all the principles of good curriculum design (see chapters 2 through 7).

- Do: Create a project model and put the plan into operation long enough to gather significant data. It is during the Do phase of the PDSA cycle that benchmarks and benchmarking are used in the curriculum change process. A benchmark is an industrial standard (a high-water mark to shoot for) that represents the best of school performance. It is the ultimate goal that, given no constraints, every school would attempt to achieve.

Benchmarking is the process whereby a school monitors its students' actual performance, records the level of achievement, and uses it as the starting point to work toward continuous improvement. Benchmarking does not involve setting numerical goals (used in traditional curriculum design and development), using the document for a period of time (usually around five years), and revising it based on performance. Instead, the revision is information driven and continuous as opposed to being time driven.

- Study: Study the results using various improvement tools that will gather data, analyze results, and help you to make accurate predictions.
- Act: The results of the study phase will determine how the school acts. It may discontinue the planned change completely if it finds it does not work. It may adjust and continue to study. Or, it may broaden the application of successful project models.

The power of the PDSA cycle in planned curriculum change is that it is a reasonable answer to the parents' position: "Implement any change you want, but don't experiment with my kid." Unlike business and industry, schools cannot experiment without causing possible harm to a human being. However, as in all social science, there is a need for education to continually change. To think otherwise is medieval. Therefore, making initial small changes in both time and number of students involved is a feasible approach. It allows education to implement planned change without fear of irreparable damage to a student or students, because even if the planned change does not work, the school system will be able to rectify any damage done to students involved. Most elementary and secondary educational plans involve a thirteen-year process. It can be argued rationally that a semester or less cannot do irreparable damage to a student.

Since education is a human process, it cannot experiment without using human beings; and, of course, these human beings are students. But education needs to experiment. It must experiment to make improvements. The PDSA cycle, using project models, offers a feasible approach to educational research without harming students. Politically, it offers the best approach to parents' fear of experimentation.

PROFOUND KNOWLEDGE AND CURRICULUM PROCESS

Profound knowledge, as defined by Deming,[7] has much to offer the planned curriculum change process. According to Deming, profound knowledge has four components. The first is knowledge of how a system operates. This means the knowledge of the interdependence of functions with their subprocesses and of the organization with its people. In relation to curriculum process, this specifically refers to articulation and coordination (K–12) regarding communication and document format. Most important of all, it refers to a school system consistently reacting to the internal and external quality question. That question is, "How can I make your job more effective?"

The second component is the knowledge of the theory of variation. This is the understanding of the difference between common and special cause. In relation to curriculum, variation must come in giving students who need it more time to learn. Further, the required curriculum must be only basic skill competencies. Variation in curriculum applies in the specialization phase of curriculum. Ranking, failing, and evaluation also must take into account the theory of variation.

The third component is a theory of knowledge, which holds that in order to continuously grow, an organization needs to look to the outside for additional knowledge. This is illustrated in curriculum change and curriculum development through the use of working models in the research phase of curriculum design. The theory of profound knowledge is also evident in the use of curriculum consortiums. When teachers from different school districts work together in curriculum development or revision, they are tapping the knowledge of teachers outside their own school district.

The fourth component is knowledge of psychology. This knowledge centers on the role of teachers in the curriculum process. Ownership and the accompanying responsiveness depend on having a psychological investment in the process and making a commitment of applying systemic thinking to a people-oriented approach. To meet these psychological conditions, curriculum change must involve teachers as major stakeholders from start to finish of any planned curriculum change.

The Paradigm Shift Question

Now we turn to the key question that should guide the school as it contemplates planned curriculum change. The question, referred to by Barker[8] as the paradigm shift question, is: What is it that is impossible today, but if it could be done would fundamentally change the way your school provides curriculum design and implementation? Think about that question. Ponder over it. Play with it continuously. From the discussions of the paradigm shift question will come possibilities for substantive change. That's what schools need in working toward planned curriculum change—substantive change.

Schools do not need cosmetic changes that do not alter the system. That is tinkering, something schools already do too much of. The schools that constantly address the paradigm shift question are the ones that can see the endless possibilities of the future. These schools will be ready to pioneer the future, a future limited only by the constraints placed upon curriculum by the traditions and paradigms of the present. Some of them are worth keeping. In fact, it is imperative that schools preserve what is good about current curriculum practice. But other curriculum components need discarding through the proper use of the paradigm shift question. Then, through the processes defined in this chapter, systemic change can occur.

Dimensions of Change

In attempting to lead curriculum change, leaders must be careful to not assume that content change initiative and implementation strategies will occur smoothly.

Curriculum change begins with content. At this stage, the discussion and decision making centers around philosophy and cognitive concerns. Once consensus is achieved, the second step is implementation.

The consensus achieved on content may or may not survive the implementation process. For example, teachers who supported the philosophical basis for the planned change may decide that, upon implementation, they no longer support the change because of its effect on their teaching function.

This interaction effect will produce four different organizational cultural effects:

1. If the change initiative (content) and the implementation strategies (process) are both positive, then implementation will be successful, and stands a good chance of augmentation.
2. If the change initiative (content) is positive, but the implementation strategies (process) is met with behavioral resistance, the change will be undermined by those charged with implementing the change.
3. If there is resistance both cognitively and affectively at the change initiative, but is supported at the implementation stage, change will prevail in some form, although it may not be exactly as envisioned at the change initiative.
4. If there is cognitive and affective resistance at the change initiative and behavioral resistance at the implementation stage, then immunity will be the effect and the change will not occur in any form.
5. Therefore, the curriculum leader must be knowledgeable of how the interaction of resistance and facilitation with the content and process of change occurs. Specifically, the curriculum leader must never embark upon a change that does not have support and consensus when the change is initiated.

Success

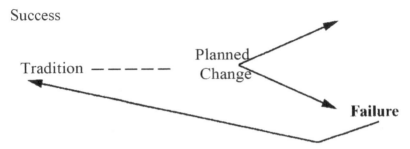

Figure 8.4. "Back to Tradition" Rule

6. Once that support and consensus is assured, the curriculum leader must closely monitor the implementation strategies so that behavioral resistance, based on cultural attitudes and behavior, is addressed and overcome through sound leadership principles as defined within this chapter.

"BACK TO TRADITION" RULE

The "back to tradition" rule holds that if a planned change fails, the organization will automatically revert to the tradition that the planned change replaced. This will occur even if there is no data to support the tradition (see figure 8.4).

NOTES

1. J. Barker, *Discovering the Future: The Business of Paradigms* [videotape] (Burnsville, MN: ChartHouse Learning, 1990).

2. Ibid.

3. W. W. Scherkenbach, *The Deming Route to Quality and Productivity: Roadmaps and Roadblocks* (Washington, D.C.: Ceep Press, 1991), 10.

4. Barker, *Discovering the Future*.

5. D. Halberstam, *The Reckoning* (New York: Avon Books, 1986), 746.

6. Wong, Harry K., Britton, Ted, and Ganzer, Tom. *What the World can Teach us About New Teacher Induction*, Phi Delta Kappan; January, 2005.

7. W. E. Deming, *The New Economics for Industry, Government, Education* (Cambridge, MA: MIT Press, 1993), 94.

8. Barker, *Discovering the Future*.

REFERENCE

Ornstein, A., Pajak, E., and Ornstein, S. (2015). *Contemporary issues in curriculum* (6th ed.). Boston: Pearson Education Publishing.

Chapter 9

Correlating Curriculum Design with How the Brain Learns

It has been said of educators that we are the only people who work with the brain every day and do not know much about it. That is a serious charge, but it contains at least some elements of truth. Teaching has not been a reflective profession; it has tended to be an art form. However, with the recent advancement of medical technology, education now has information that could move teaching more toward science.

When schools design and implement curriculum, they should ensure that the facts about how the brain learns are incorporated in the total curriculum process. Some of the facts and principles about how the brain learns apply to curriculum design. Others apply to curriculum implementation. When applied holistically, they ensure that the student is in a school that is given the best opportunity to acquire, remember, and utilize knowledge.

HOW THE BRAIN LEARNS: IMPLICATIONS FOR CURRICULUM DESIGN AND IMPLEMENTATION

The Three Domains of Learning

The brain has three centers or domains of learning: affective, psychomotor, and cognitive.[1]

- The affective domain is the most powerful. It is within this domain that the brain senses physical and emotional danger. Physical danger has the highest priority of the brain's senses. Emotional danger has the second priority.

- The psychomotor domain greatly influences memory. The kinesthetic experiences produced by this domain are the basis of the long-held knowledge that people learn by doing.
- The cognitive domain has the lowest priority within the human brain. However, it lasts the longest, therefore having the most endurance.

Knowledge about these domains of learning has the following implications for curriculum design and implementation:

- Since the affective domain is the most powerful, emotion-based thinking will take precedence over pure cognition. Therefore, curriculum implementation must provide the students the opportunity for affective expression. For example, instead of talking about a topic such as racism, the curriculum implementation should provide the students the opportunity to write poetry or prose on how they feel about it.
- Since cognitive learning lasts the longest and has the most endurance, it should make up the significant portion of curriculum design. Because of its low priority in brain functioning in comparison to the affective domain, curriculum implementation must find ways of eliminating the affective needs so that the cognitive domain can be effectively utilized.
- Since emotional danger takes precedence over cognitive processing, to design curriculum that puts the student at a frustration level will prevent cognitive processing from occurring. It naturally follows that curriculum implementation that creates emotional danger in the perception of the student will eliminate the possibility of effective cognitive processing by the student or students who are experiencing the emotional danger. Keep in mind that the emotional danger being discussed is either real or perceived by the student. It matters not which one is really present. If the student perceives that he is in any emotional danger, that brain processing will prevail even if the emotional danger is only imagined (See figure 9.1).
- The presence of physical danger is also a blocker of cognitive functioning. This is not a curriculum design problem but a curriculum implementation problem. Anyone attempting to understand why schools with high incidence of violence have low achievement need only look at this simple principle about how the brain learns. Schools in which students feel physically threatened should devote their curriculum design and implementation time to improving the environment to eliminate the danger to students. The best curriculum design and implementation program in the world won't work if the students feel physically threatened.

The current school reformers who base school reform solely on test scores ignore this principle about how the brain learns. Their answer to school

How the Brain Processes Information

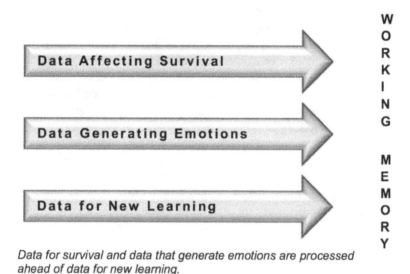

Data for survival and data that generate emotions are processed ahead of data for new learning.

Figure 9.1.   How the Brain Processes Information

problems is higher standards in curriculum and accountability based on norm-referenced tests. Neither of these has a chance of occurring until the physical dangers to students are removed from the school environment.

The discussion of this topic points up the interdependence of the total school operation. Schools must stop thinking of curriculum design and implementation in isolation from the rest of the school operation, even the noninstructional services such as the building, transportation, and leisure time. They are all part of the system that provides inputs, throughputs, and outputs to one another. Effective curriculum design and implementation will be affected by every operation the school is involved in. Systemic thinking must be utilized in curriculum design and implementation.

- Because kinesthetic experiences help with memory, curriculum design objectives should indicate significant student activity. However, it is in curriculum implementation that teachers can assure the presence of active student participation in the learning process. It is in this domain that inter-active technology should play a significant part. It is imperative that future curriculum design and implementation includes the use of computers, inter-active videos, and other technologies that are totally dependent on active student participation.

- Humor makes the brain better able to learn.[2] Therefore, teachers should use humor to stimulate the brain prior to working with cognition. This suggestion runs contrary to many traditions about the classroom. Such practices as "don't smile till Thanksgiving" and "a quiet classroom is a good classroom" do not lend themselves to the use of humor. But the fact is, humor will help learning. So educators need to find a way to make use of the fact. A quick story, a funny cartoon on a transparency, or good interpersonal communication skills are some ways to incorporate humor into the classroom without losing control of the students. Good teachers are already doing it. The practice just needs to become more widespread.
- Practice makes learning permanent but not perfect. Repetition in both curriculum design and implementation will not guarantee competence. The most important thing about any student practice activity is that it is accompanied by measures to verify its accuracy. Therefore, in curriculum implementation, it is imperative that practice be monitored to make sure that it is moving the student toward perfection and not just permanence. But perfect practice does make learning permanent.
- People are born with the ability to think. Curriculum design and implementation should concentrate on how to teach people to organize their thinking.

Information Enters the Brain through the Senses

Information about the environment enters our brain through the five senses: sight, hearing, touch, taste, and smell. However, in relation to learning for students K–12, the senses are not of equal importance. Consider the following information compiled by David Sousa.[3]

Obviously, people have a distinct learning preference or style.

Knowledge about sensory learning preferences has the following implications for curriculum design and implementation:

- Curriculum design and implementation should reflect the obvious preference of most people to visual learning. It is in the implementation function that the visual preference could be accommodated. It seems almost unbelievable that this principle of learner preference has not made its way into the classroom. The chief obstacles seem to be the tradition of opposing

Table 9.1. Human Senses and Learning Preferences

Senses	Learning Preferences for K–12 Students (%)
Sight	47
Hearing	19
Touch	34

change and the cost involved in providing a classroom that accommodates the sensory learning preferences.
- Change is the most common thing in society. However, education is the only institution that has not experienced a systemic change. The classroom looks a lot like it did at the turn of the twentieth century. In curriculum implementation, teachers should increase visual and kinesthetic activities.
- Make the students put their senses to work. Remember the old Chinese proverb: "He who explains, learns." It is not the teachers' senses that are important here; it is the students' senses. Put them to use. Identify each student's preference and try to maximize them within the constraints of a twenty- to thirty-student classroom.

Experience Is a Powerful Influence on Learning

When new information comes to the brain, its perceptual register either keeps the information or screens it out in milliseconds based on experience. So, never underestimate the power that experience has in learning.

Knowledge about the influence of experience on learning has the following implications for curriculum design and implementation:

- In curriculum design, the implication is that articulation is important in meeting this brain characteristic. Poorly articulated curriculum may be confusing and frustrating to the student. His earlier experiences in the curriculum may have left him poorly prepared for the current learning expectations, thus adversely affecting his learning.
- In curriculum implementation, this principle of how the brain learns calls for good pre-assessment procedures and practices. By doing pre-assessment, the teacher can become knowledgeable about this particular aspect of the students' prior learning and thus be better prepared to meet their cognitive and affective needs. Pre-assessment is especially important if earlier experience has left the student with a negative feeling about the subject. If the student has a negative feeling, previous discussion about the priority of the learning domains tells us that until the affective concerns have been addressed, the cognitive needs cannot be addressed.

The Brain Has Many Kinds of Memory

The human brain has three kinds of memory: short-term, working, and long-term.

- Short-term memory is temporary. The perceptual register in the brain stem either keeps information or screens it out in a matter of milliseconds. The short-term memory lasts about one minute. The brain works subconsciously in keeping or screening out information.

- Working memory is still temporary, but it is conscious. The capacity of the working memory is age dependent. In people under the age of fourteen, the brain can deal with only five items at a time. Above the age of fourteen, this number increases to seven items at a time.
- The brain uses two criteria when moving information to long-term memory[4]:

  - Does the information make sense?
  - Does the information have meaning?

The brain has multiple, unlimited storage areas for long-term storage. The capacity is unlimited, and the time limit is a lifetime. There are many pathways to long-term memory. Forgetting occurs when the brain loses the pathway to the long-term storage.

Each of us has a cognitive belief system that can be defined as our view of the world and how the world works. The cognitive belief system is unique to each person. Deep within the cognitive belief system is the individual's self-concept. While the cognitive belief system portrays the way a person sees the world, the self-concept describes the way a person sees themselves in that world. Self-concept is formed by experiences. If these experiences have been negative about certain information, the person will tend to reject learning opportunities in this area.

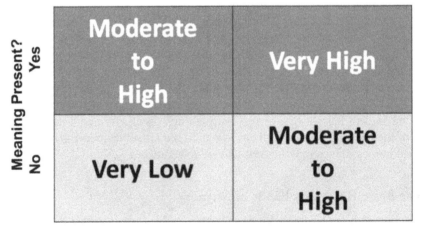

Figure 9.2.   Effect of Sense and Meaning on Long Term Memory

The brain has a psychological and physiological cycle that is high until mid-day but gets low in the mid-afternoon. These cycles also affect the attention span. For people younger than fourteen, the normal attention span is five to ten minutes. For people fourteen and older, the normal attention span is ten to twenty minutes. Needless to say, the attention span is lengthened through increased interest, motivation, the changing of learning modes, and intervening activity.

Long-term memory can be tested only through unannounced assessment. If a person knows the test is coming and what it covers, they will cram or engage in other activities that will affect the test score and, therefore, measure more than long-term memory.

Knowledge about the three kinds of memory has the following implications for curriculum design and implementation:

- Since self-concept is located within the cognitive domain, curriculum design and implementation should stop working with this human need within the affective domain. Those "touchy-feely" activities may have value but, according to the research on how the brain learns, they will not improve a person's self-concept. The only way to improve a learner's self-concept is through successful experiences within the cognitive domain. The person must experience success so that his perceptual register will allow information entry into the brain and not filter it out immediately because of previous negative experience. Teachers cannot talk a student into a positive self-concept. The student must gain it through successful experiences.
- The short-term memory has little relevance to long-term learning.

However, since it is the first entry of information into the brain (see figure 9.3), it is important that any new information presented to students be powerful enough in content and delivery that the short-term memory won't kick it out.[5] Remember, the brain makes this decision in milliseconds. The most significant fact is, if the brain decides to screen the information out, it is out. And when it is out, it is gone, never to be retrieved. Therefore, the information cannot move to working memory. Teachers are sometimes losing students at this point.

- The brain uses two criteria when deciding whether to screen out or keep information: (a) Does it make sense? and (b) Does it have meaning? Curriculum design needs to address the question, "Does it make sense?" If the curriculum design is based on meaningful content, properly articulated, and clearly stated, then the curriculum design has a chance of convincing the student that they can understand this information.

Brain Processing Model

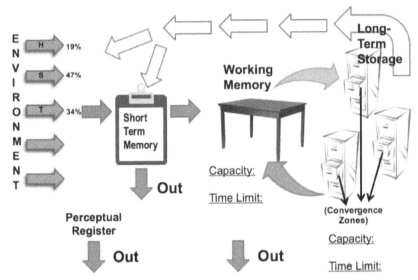

Figure 9.3.   Brain Processing Model. Based on Model by David A. Sousa, Rev. 11192

The question, "Does this information have meaning?" is usually asked by the student in one of the following forms: "So what?" or "What does this mean to me in my life?" Although curriculum design can assist in meeting this individual need, it is in the area of curriculum implementation that the need is best met.

What this fact about how the brain learns is telling educators is that before teaching information, answer the question, "so what?" There is a difference between beginning a history unit on the French Revolution by immediately launching into a chronological presentation of who went to the guillotine and beginning by saying that the French Revolution is the first attempt at democracy in Western Europe, and that the results of the French Revolution affected the history of Europe, America, and the world for the next hundred years. The message the teacher is trying to convey to the students is that the very way they live today was partly created by the French Revolution.

This teacher task would be easier if the curriculum content was the Civil War, or word processing, or auto mechanics. It would be harder in algebra class. Regardless of whether the curricular content is easily associated with the students' lives or very remote to their current existence, the chances of the information reaching the students' long-term memory are increased if the teacher can successfully address the students' question, "How does this have meaning to me?"

- Teachers, in curriculum implementation, must address the question of the brain's capacity to remember related information. The grouping of any coherent items of information so that we can remember it as easily as a single item is called chunking.[6] Recall that individuals younger than fourteen can deal with five items or chunks at a time (plus or minus two), and that individuals fourteen and older can deal with seven items or chunks at a time (plus or minus two). Following is a quick demonstration of how to use chunking in teaching.

  a. In a few seconds, try to memorize the following numbers in the order given: After five seconds, look away and then write the numbers down in proper order.

7419628

How did you do? Probably OK. Let's do it again using chunking. I'm going to give you seven different numbers in two chunks. Ready? Go.

732 6054

Most people do better when the numbers are grouped in two chunks. It looks like a telephone number. Instead of memorizing seven numbers, you memorized two numbers of multiple digits. This is a pattern that is part of your experience.

For ten numbers, the same principle would apply. You simply add the "area code." So if you are dealing with ten numbers, use three chunks like this:

513 732 6076

  b. The capacity of the brain is increased by using association. Let's try another demonstration exercise. Once again, try to memorize the following letters in the proper order. Do it in a few seconds, look away, and write them down on a piece of paper. Ready? Go. NFLCBSATAT

Now, do it again with chunking. Ready? Go. NFL   CBS   ATAT
You probably did better by chunking because you can associate these three chunks with information that is part of your experience: a major sports league, a television network, and a major American business.[7]

  c. How learning experiences are sequenced in curriculum delivery can increase retention. To demonstrate this principle, please do the following exercise. You will need a pencil and a timer. Set the timer for twelve seconds. When you start the timer, look at the following list of ten words.

Table 9.2.

Sarah	1.	Nuts	6.
House	2.	Here	7.
Go	3.	Myself	8.
Buy	4.	And	9.
Me	5.	Go	10.

When the timer sounds, cover the ten words and write as many of the ten words as you remember on the lines to the right of the list. Write each word on the line that represents its position on the list; that is, the first word on the first line, the second word on the second line, and so on. So, for example, if you don't remember the sixth word but you do remember the seventh word, leave the sixth word blank and write the seventh word on the tenth line. Ready? Set the timer and go.

Most people who do this exercise remember the first three to five words and the last two words (lines 9 and 10) but have difficulty with the middle words (lines 6 through 8). There is a reason for this, and that reason (described in the next section) has important implications for curriculum implementation.

PRIMACY-RECENCY EFFECT

The pattern in remembering the word list is a common phenomenon known as the primacy-regency effect. In a learning experience, such as a daily lesson, we tend to remember best that which comes first and remember second best that which comes last. We tend to remember least that which comes in the middle or just past the middle.[8] The application of the primacy-recency effect to curriculum implementation leads to the concept of prime time and down time for learning. The first and best prime time is the beginning of the learning episode. The second and next-best prime time is the end of the learning episode, and the down time is the middle and just past the middle of the learning episode (see figure 9.4).

By referring to figure 9.5, you can see how these prime times and down time look for lessons ranging from twenty to eighty minutes. This figure clearly demonstrates that curriculum implementation is more effective if presented in smaller chunks in relation to class presentations and activities. It would be better to do two twenty-minute lessons instead of one forty-minute lesson. It would also be more productive to do three lessons of twenty-five to thirty minutes as opposed to one eighty-minute lesson.

The most important message from the primacy-recency effect for curriculum implementation is to determine the top learning priority for the learning

Lesson Length

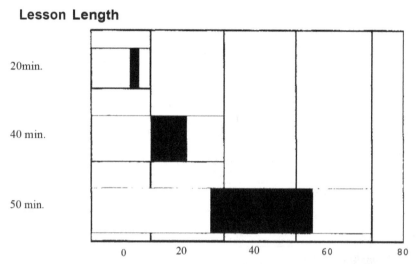

Figure 9.4.   Approximate Ratio of Prime Time to Down Time during Learning Episode

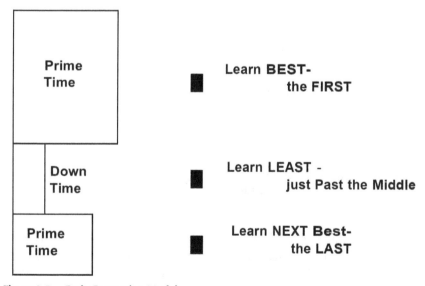

Figure 9.5.   Brain Processing Model

episode and place it during the first prime time. Some common instructional practices in use today ignore the primacy-recency effect, thus reducing potential learning. Table 9.3 illustrates lesson planning that violates the primacy-recency effect.

Table 9.3. Lesson Planning That Violates the Primacy-Recency Effect

Misuse of Prime Time I—Beginning of Class

Prime Time I	*Activities*

1. Handing out papers
2. Taking attendance
3. Checking seating
4. Making announcements
5. Lecturing reports or small group work that does not represent new learning

Misuse of Down Time—Middle and Just Past Middle of Class

Downtime	*Activity*

1. Conducting most important part of new learning (lecture, question-and-answer, film, etc.)

Misuse of Prime Time II—End of Class

Prime Time II	*Activities*

1. Winding-down activities
2. Ending class on down note
3. No culminating activities
4. No review of key information
5. Using for study hall
6. No attention to assignment or important exit information

Knowledge about the primacy-recency effect has the following implications for curriculum design and implementation:

- The facts about the brain's attention span and time limits has significant ramifications for curriculum design and implementation. Based on current curriculum design practices, one could assume that the attention span is forty-five minutes to an hour. That is the time frame within which most high school classes are scheduled. It also corresponds to many elementary learning blocks.

The instructional schedule is based on other factors such as state standards on time, organizational structure, transportation concerns, and lunch schedules. Therefore, the design is not likely to undergo a systemic change. However, within the curriculum design, curriculum implementation could change to correlate with how the brain functions with regard to attention spans and time limits. For students younger than fourteen, lesson plans should reflect the need to change learning modes to coincide with the five- to ten-minute attention span. For students over fourteen, lesson plans should reflect the ten to twenty-minute attention span. Remember that these are average attention spans that will vary with individuals as well as with interest and motivation.

This characteristic of the brain can be accommodated in the classroom by constantly varying the learning mode to keep interest and motivation. Rehearsal in curriculum design and implementation involves the use of chunking. Chunking is a learned skill, not a function of intelligence. It is usually done through pairing, selecting, or integrating. Central to getting information into the long-term memory is the practice of rehearsal.

The assignment of sense and meaning to new learning can only occur if the learner has adequate time to process and reprocess it. This continuing reprocessing is called rehearsal, and it is critical in transferring information from working memory to long-term memory. The first factor to consider in rehearsal is how much time to devote to it. The second decision is which type of rehearsal should be carried out: rote or elaborative. In answering these two questions, remember that their importance lies in the fact that there is almost no long-term retention without rehearsal.

Rote rehearsal is a type of rehearsal that is used when the learner needs to remember and store information exactly as it is entered into working memory. This is not complex learning. We use rote memory for telephone numbers, poems, lyrics of songs, multiplication tables, or other facts involving steps.

Elaborative rehearsal is a type of rehearsal that is used when it is not necessary to store information exactly as learned, but it is more important to associate the new learning with prior learning to detect relationships. This is a more complex learning process.

Students who use only or predominantly rote rehearsal fail to make the associations or discover the relationships that only elaborate rehearsal can provide. Also, they continue to believe that learning is merely recalling information as learned rather than generating new ideas, concepts, and solutions.

In curriculum implementation, schools need to move away from too much rote rehearsal and toward more elaborative rehearsal. Currently, rote rehearsal makes up 80 percent of rehearsal activities and elaborative rehearsal makes up the other 20 percent. Curriculum implementation would be better served if these numbers were reversed. This is not to say there shouldn't be rote rehearsal, but its use is too widespread in areas where elaborative rehearsal is called for. Rote rehearsal is also too much of an end in itself when it should be the prerequisite learning activity to elaborative rehearsal.

When deciding how to use rehearsal in the implementation of curriculum, teachers should consider the intent of the learning outcome and choose the rehearsal that meets the need. Remember that rehearsal contributes to but does not guarantee that information will be transferred to long-term memory. Also remember that there is almost no long-term memory storage without some type of rehearsal.

Cramming is a form of chunking.[9] Students do it effectively before exams. What educators should remember is that cramming is dealing mostly with the working memory. In many cases, long-term memory is not utilized, nor does any of the information tested reach long-term memory. Therefore, a curriculum design and implementation system that includes only announced exams does not measure long-term memory. If a school system wished to administer an examination that would best assess the long-term memory of the students, an unannounced test would be the most effective means. By giving the exam unannounced, the student does not have the benefit of short-term and working memory information accessed through cramming.

The elimination of announced assessment procedures is not being advocated here. But if a school system wishes to assess the long-term memory of the student body, an unannounced exam is the best evaluation method. This discussion does not address the issue of what kind of unannounced exam should be given. That is a test and measurement issue requiring a lengthy discussion not covered in this chapter. A paper-and-pencil test is one type of exam, and many other types of assessment would also measure long-term memory. The point being emphasized here is that, if the school wishes to measure long-term memory, unannounced exams are the most valid measure.

Skimming Information Is a Useless Learning Activity for Working or Long-Term Memory

Based on the facts about how the brain learns that have been presented in the chapter so far, it is obvious that skimming classroom material is of no value to working or long-term memory.

Knowledge about skimming information has the following implications for curriculum design and implementation: Curriculum design and implementation should implement abandonment by using what is sometimes referred to as "postholing." Refer to figure 9.6, which shows the difference between abandonment through postholing and skimming. In this American history course, the figure shows how the course was taught through the use of a chronological time line. This approach would require significant skimming. The figure then shows how the course could be taught by postholing certain key concepts for intensive attention and then connecting the postholes. In the chronological time line, all concepts are given equal value in terms of time and emphasis. In postholing, the key concepts are given more time and emphasis.

Approach 1: Chronological Military History of America 1492–Present
Approach 2: Postholing the Military History of America: Emphasizing Key
  Concepts with Connectors
Colonization Civil War Industrialization WWI WWII Present

Learning Pyramid

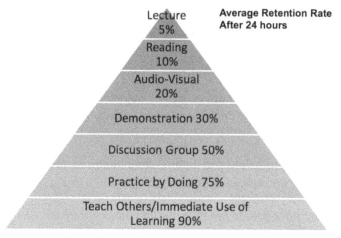

Sousa, David A. How the Brain Learns, Virginia, NASSP

Figure 9.6.   Learning Pyramid

Note: Connectors are defined as the information needed to understand the posthole being taught. The term does not imply that all historical events occurring between the succeeding postholes will be taught. That would be skimming. Using connectors means that only the information needed to teach the current posthole is a part of the curriculum design and implementation.

Episodic Memory

This is the autobiographical memory. A person does not have any control over this memory. One cannot decide to store or not store. Its significance to learning is that it lends itself to "hand on" learning that teaches to the episodic memory. Using it in curriculum and instruction is motivating to the student because it is personal, thus making it meaningful. Also, it can lend more relevance to the topic, because it is or was a part of the learner's life.

CREATING LEARNING THAT LASTS

(What Neuroscience tells us works for improved long-term memory.)

The learning pyramid (see figure 9.6), based on the research of Sousa, shows how the current instructional methods produce better memory retention. The obvious message is that the more engaged the learner, the more likelihood of working memory retention.

Research findings from neuroscience about how we learn and how to optimize the function of memory can be categorized under the following.

Attention—Generation—Emotions—Spacing

With just the right amount of attention, generation, emotions, and spacing, learners intensely activate their hippocampus, which creates deep circuits for easy retrieval of data.

A. Attention—"Distractions and multi-tasking inhibit the ability to focus sufficiently to learn something new."

Following are principles to optimize the attention of learners:

1. Full attention is necessary for the hippocampus of the brain to activate.
2. Cell phones, iPads, and other technology create divided attention.
3. Undivided attention is needed for quality of attention and thus memory retention.
4. Online learning contains inherent distractions.
5. Relevance is so important in creating memory: the learner needs to see the value or potential reward.
6. Therefore, make learning situations as real and personal as possible.
7. Simulations are good because they produce arousal due to role playing.
8. Alertness is affected negatively by threat; positively by challenge.
9. The social brain maximizes attention, so teachers should strive to create the learning community.
10. A significant finding in the brain research of Gardner (1) is that brain's attention span is mature by the age of twelve, which means that learners beyond the age of twelve who are having difficulty with attention span is due to behavioral issues, and not physiology.

B. Generation—"Memories are made up of vast webs of data from across the brain all linked together. Information is not expressly stored in the hippocampus as discrete memories like in a hard drive."

Following are principles to maximize generation learning:

1. Use association in curriculum and instruction through interdisciplinary and integrated learning.

2. Remember that repetition has limited impact on creating lasting memory.
3. Personalize learning, thus creating meaning.
4. Teach fewer concepts at a deeper level.
5. Use elaborative rehearsal as opposed to rote rehearsal.
6. Presented with data, allow the learner to formulate, organize, and add personal experience to the learning content.
7. Questioning the learner triggers retrieval of the recently learned content and improves long-term memory.

C. Emotions—Emotions enhance memory in two ways:

First, emotional content is thought to grab the attention of the individual and, hence, help to focus attention on the emotional event or stimulus.

Second, it is known that emotion leads to activation of a brain structure called the amygdala, which sits directly in front of the hippocampus and can help to signal to the hippocampus that a particular event is salient, and thus increase the effectiveness of encoding.

Emotions can be triggered by negative or positive forces.

Negative emotions are stimulated by the following:

1. Fear or threat (examples are assessment tools and reports)
2. Training programs focusing on the negatives of the presenter instead of their strengths

Positive emotions are stimulated by the following:

1. Increasing people's sense of status, certainty, autonomy, relatedness, or fairness
2. Positive feedback
3. Making learning events enjoyable
4. Creating positive social connections and experiences among the learners.

D. Spacing—"It has been known for some time that distributing learning over time is better than cramming learning into one long study session, and leads to better long-term memory."

Learning Event + Small Delay + Testing = Best Results

Repeated testing is superior to repeated studying in the formation of maximum long-term memory.

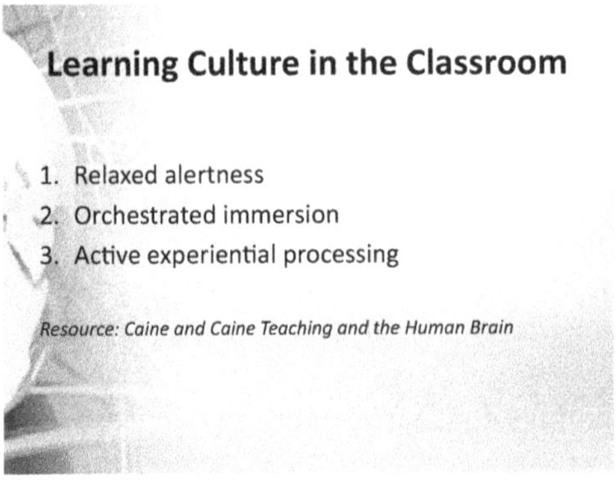

Learning Culture in the Classroom

1. Relaxed alertness
2. Orchestrated immersion
3. Active experiential processing

Resource: Caine and Caine Teaching and the Human Brain

Figure 9.7.   Leading Structural/Cultural Change

CLASSROOM LEARNING CULTURE

Caine and Caine's research demonstrated that classroom instruction that contains relaxed alertness, orchestrated immersion, and active experiential processing increases the likelihood of memory retention.

Relaxed alertness means that the learners are engaged in the learning process but are not threatened or fearful of the classroom culture.

Orchestrated immersion means that the teacher has guided the lesson in such a way as to immerse the learners in the planned learning outcomes. This is the phase that the expertise of the teacher is utilized so that the knowledge level of the learners is being challenged.

Active experiential processing means that the learners utilize kinesthetic activities to engage themselves into the pursuit of the learning outcomes, either individually or in teams.

CONCLUDING REMARKS

The last twenty-five years have produced a boon in brain research that was not available to educators when many of the practices that determine current curriculum design and implementation were established. Medical technology such as CT scans, PET scans, and MRIs have produced information that educators can use to make curriculum design and implementation more scientific. The education profession must make use of current knowledge about the brain so that myths can be dispelled and replaced by new scientific facts about the brain and how it learns. Let us practice one of the facts that the recent research has proven: when it comes to the brain, use it or lose it.

IMPLICATIONS FOR CURRICULUM LEADERSHIP

Gardner's research on brain cell development, key building blocks for brain cells, and toxins and habits that kill brain cells have significant implications for curriculum, instruction, and school organizational issues.

The following chart on brain cell development has significant implications for early childhood education:

A. 50 percent by age four
B. 35 percent more by age eight
C. 15 percent more by age ten

In relation to key building blocks for brain cells, Gardner lists the following as imperative:

A. Oxygen
B. Water
C. Nutrition

It is within nutrition that schools can have a positive effect, through breakfast and lunch programs to ensure that all students are not hungry to the point of being unable to learn.

Gardner also points out the value of red, orange, yellow, and green vegetables in brain growth. School food services can assist in seeing this need is met. Gardner also identifies the three toxins/habits that kill brain cells:

A. Oxidants
B. Drugs/Alcohol
C. Poor Nutrition

NOTES

1. Michael Gazzaniga, "The Split Brain in Man," *Scientific American* (August 1967): 24–29.
2. David A. Sousa, "How the Brain Learns: New Insights for Educators," Phi Delta Kappa Workshop (November 30, 1995), South Bend, Ind.
3. David A. Sousa, *How the Brain Learns: A Classroom Teacher's Guide* (Reston, VA: National Association of Secondary Principals, 1995), 10.
4. Ibid., 15–18.
5. Ibid., II.
6. Ibid., 49–51.

7. E. J. Thomas, "The Variation of Memory with Time for Information Appearing during a Lecture," *Studies in Adult Education* (April 1972): 57–62.
8. Sousa, "How the Brain Learns: New Insights for Educators."
9. M. C. Hunter, *Mastery Teaching* (El Segundo, CA: T.I.P. Publications, 1982).

REFERENCES

Berlinger, D., and Pinero, U. C. (1985). "How Memory Works: Implications for Teachers." *Instructor*, 94: 14–15.
Bloom, E., and Lazerson A. 1985. *Brain, Mind, and Matter*, 2nd ed. New York: Freeman.
Buzan, T. (1983). *Use Both Sides of Your Brain*. New York: Dutton.
Caine, Geoffrey. (1999). *Best Practices for Brain-Compatible Classrooms* [video recording]. Arlington, IL: Skyline Professional Development.
Caine, Geoffrey, and Renate N. Caine. (1997). *Education on the Edge of Possibility*. Alexandria, VA: Association for Supervision and Curriculum Development.
Caine, Geoffrey, Renate N. Caine, and Sam Crowell. (1994). *Mind shifts: A Brain-Based Process for Restructuring Schools and Renewing Education*. Tucson, AZ: Zephyr Press.
Caine, Renate N., and Geoffrey Caine. (1991). *Making Connections: Teaching and the Human Brain*. Alexandria, VA: Association for Supervision and Curriculum Development.
Fogarty, R., and J. Bellanca. (1989). *Patterns for Thinking, Patterns for Transfer*. Palatine, IL: Skylight Publishing.
Gardner, H. (1983). *Frames of Mind: The Theory of Multiple Intelligences*. New York: Basic Books.
Grady, M. P. (1984). *Teaching and Brain Research*. New York: Longman.
Nummela, R. M., and T. Rosengran. (1986). "What's Happening in Students' Brains May Redefine Teaching." *Educational Leadership* 43: 49–53.
Orstein, R., and R. F. Thompson. (1986). *The Amazing Brain*. Boston: Houghton Mifflin.
Sylwester, Robert. (1995). *A Celebration of Neurons: An Educator's Guide to the Human Brain*. Alexandria, VA: Association for Supervision and Curriculum Development.
Winkles, J. (1986). "Achievement, Understanding, and Transfer in a Learning Hierarchy." *American Educational Research Journal* 2: 65.

Chapter 10

Technology and Curriculum Development

IMPLICATIONS OF TECHNOLOGY FOR CURRICULUM

Before the advent of modern technology for curriculum, school systems based curriculum development on a set sequence and review cycle. A typical five-year cycle would look like table 10.1:

This cyclical process was dictated more by human resource and logistical problems than by sound educational principles or the needs of learners. The need for curriculum revision does not follow logical time patterns. A five-year cycle may work effectively for one subject but be inadequate for another. New knowledge within a learning discipline may occur at any time. This new knowledge may be so vital that it needs to be incorporated into the curriculum immediately. In the paper technology era, this was possible but difficult. It required time and resulted mostly in inserts to the current curriculum document. However, the focus in either case remains on the delivery of content and not on student learning and the needs associated with such learning.

With technology, such revisions based on new, vital knowledge can be incorporated immediately. It is feasible with technology to move from paper curriculum documents to curriculum "online." However, the curriculum process itself can be adjusted using technology, creating a learning-centric mind-set at all levels of education. The advantage of such a change is that the curriculum process would be available to all participants in the learning process—teachers, students, parents, administration, and community. And, of course, curriculum revisions could take place more continuously than was possible using paper technology or with the mind-set established by the paper focused curriculum process.

The human resource capacity might continue to dictate curriculum revision based on five-year review cycles. There can be the belief that not enough

Table 10.1. Curriculum Development Timeline

2003–2004	Language arts and math	2008–2009
2004–2005	Science and social studies	2009–2010
2005–2006	Fine arts	2010–2011
2006–2007	Foreign languages	2011–2012
2007–2008	All others	2012–2013

quality time, nor available administrative resources, exist to revise all curriculum areas every year. However, with the effective use of technology, and the technology mind-set, school systems now have the capacity to revise curriculum immediately and pervasively. Technology also has given the schools the capacity to share the planned curriculum, curriculum process, and instructional components with all the stakeholders in an ongoing manner.

TECHNOLOGY MIND-SET IN CURRICULUM AND INSTRUCTION

The goal of curriculum and instruction remains the same across the educational profession: "What can be done to allow students to learn?" The issues associated with curriculum and instruction arise when the focus of that learning, objectives and the like, enter the conversation. This section will focus on the use of technology, and the mind-set technology can bring to curriculum.

Technology plays, and will continue to play, a key role in curriculum development as trends unfold simply because there is no other manner in which to develop, implement, and manage the complicated changes that will continue to arise across the educational landscape. Technology provides a means of connecting students and teachers and the curriculum process that was not available previously. This is not the use of technology for the sake of technology, instead this is the opening of possibilities for the thought processes of how curriculum is developed, how teachers instruct, and how students learn and the ease of connection of the three. One of the largest opportunities that exists today via technology is the role technology plays in identifying the learning needs of the students and connecting them with learning resources and/or instruction. For many years in education, curricular alignment focused exclusively on learning objectives. Can a student perform this math task? Can a student demonstrate that knowledge base? Through technology, the focus can shift to learning, what is the student's learning style? How does the student demonstrate mastery of the content? What are the student's demographic factors? In each case, these are important elements to bring forward to target the resources needed for student to learn. In this way, the student's preferred learning style can be utilized in the delivery of instructions for assignments.

By means of example, what if this mind-set is taken to its full potential? Imagine the role of curriculum and instruction if the lessons of data analytics could be brought to bear fully into the curriculum process. When students and their parents shop, visit websites, or perform any of the dozens of activities that produce data that is tracked by companies. Future experiences and interactions are tailored based on the data that was collected from previous interactions. What if this mind-set and methodology was brought fully into the curriculum and instruction process? Student performance on a given activity would produce data that is shared, analyzed, and utilized to adapt future interactions to produce greater potential for the learner from each learning experience. This is the technology mind-set in action; however, some districts and schools are not prepared for such a large step. However, this does not mean the curriculum process needs to wait for future technology, the technology mind-set can move forward, first with the idea of needs assessments.

NEEDS ASSESSMENTS

There are some in education who are utilizing the same assessment and curriculum techniques that were available over seventy years ago. Even if they are utilizing technology, they are doing so within the framework established by a non-technological point of view. The foundation for a modern curriculum process has been established by many researchers to be a needs assessment.

When the term *needs assessment* is utilized, the focus of the action can vary greatly depending on the constituent to whom the question is directed. Are the needs being assessed those of the district? community? school? student? Are needs being assessed connected to the targeted outcomes for any of these groups? The technology mind-set would propose the response to this question as all of the above, rather than any single group. The connection between the groups, outcomes, and curriculum becomes the needs assessment, and the technology mind-set allows this process to flow.

Needs assessment provides a clear direction for the curriculum process through the illustration of the standards by students should be assessed while illustrating how the curriculum can be delivered and assessed. The collection of this type of information requires a broad approach informed locally and not exclusively by referencing expert generated content alone. In order to be successful, these needs assessment must be indicative of an assessment process and not simply data collection. The data analysis and adaptations that result from the analysis must be clear and easily followed. In this manner, the process can go beyond the results generated by students and approach the reasons behind the responses for the students, as individuals and as a group. Through this active process, students will no longer be treated as passive recipients of content being delivered. It is clear that students instructed by such passive means would not be able to function in the rapidly changing technology of today's global society. This type of process has been referred to by some as formative curriculum process.

As reported by Ian Clark (2015), if a formative curriculum is to be successful, the following conditions must exist:

1. Dedicated political support at all levels of government.
2. A clear and compelling expression of the conceptual framework that underpins "formative curriculum" and drives assessment practices.
3. Close collaboration between teachers, administrators, parents/caregivers, learners, and the wider community, who understand their roles in working together to engage students with the process of their own learning.
4. Practitioners approach and manage curricula transformation so that obstacles are perceived as constructive and necessary challenges.
5. The integration of summative and formative assessment activities into a functional system so that they work in concert to support and evaluate learning.

When active, such a system would enable students to meet high standards for success set for them by all members of the community. Only when the information is shared with all constituents will the performance objectives be universally clear.

REFLECTION

In order for students to garner the most success from curriculum experiences, self-reflection must play an important part. Knowledge comprehension and higher order thinking result more completely when students are allowed to actively process their learning through reflection. Students are able to understand not only what they know but also why they know and how to apply the material. The rapid response aspect of a text driven world does not preclude reflection, but it also does not increase its probability. Students today are interacting with more people, but at lesser depths of interaction than before as they expect more from the technology they use and less from others.

Curriculum leaders, as well as academic leaders, need to ensure the curriculum process establishes multiple opportunities for all involved to reflect, as individuals and groups, on the process of learning and its outcomes. These opportunities also need to assist the students in developing the skill sets necessary to practice reflection themselves, without the scaffolding of the school. However, this needs to be accomplished by academic administrators who may lack the technological knowledge and skills necessary to develop plans that attract appropriate academic interactions, but more importantly help teachers and students develop the skills to do so successfully.

Therefore, the curriculum mind-set grounded in the use of technology must also allow the teachers to develop the knowledge and skills to connect the curricular requirements to the ever-changing population with which they will work. Teachers are willing to use technology; this has been established in numerous research projects. However, they will require constantly updated support to keep their use of technologically grounded curriculum and instruction current and relevant to their students. It is only through proper training and support that teachers can be expected to integrate technology into their classes every day.

ACCOUNTABILITY AND CONNECTIVITY

The focus of curriculum too often becomes a focus on the ability of students to develop the correct responses to prompts. These testing prompts, whether teacher-made or on a standardized assessment, the answers along should not be the focus of the curriculum. The reasons behind the student responses need to be developed in order to for the curriculum to be a success. To develop the meanings behind the responses, the assessment system developed by the curriculum, which is focused through the technological mind-set, would provide in-depth ongoing assessments of student learning.

These assessments must be developed with the conception of active student participation in the learning process. Additionally, the results of these assessments, whether formative or summative, must be shared with learners, parents, and other stakeholders, allowing the learning objectives and learning performance to be transparent. This allows all involved, especially the learner, to be able to answer the question of what they can do now with the knowledge and skills they have developed.

The success of the technological mind-set and assessment on the curriculum will depend upon the direct and explicit connection and alignment between the learning outcomes, teaching/learning activities, and the assessment. The alignment of these three elements produces a consistency within the curriculum where the movement from learning outcomes as a goal toward the performance on the assessment is a clear journey. When working in concert, the learning outcomes drive the design of the curriculum, and the teaching, learning, and assessment fall into a supporting role illustrated by the experiences of the students. Therefore, planning focuses on the determination of what should be learned. It is results-driven and the primary measure of success becomes what can students do as a result of participation in a continual improvement-focused series of learning activities.

Findings of research and evaluation studies on technology in education can be derived from several sources. Here are some primary sources:

- National policy documents
- State technology plans
- A Far West Laboratory study on state technology programs
- Studies of model technology schools
- Report on the effectiveness of technology in schools[1]

The research easily points up the major problems that schools have in trying to effectively utilize technology in curriculum design and implementation. First and foremost is trying to keep up with technological advancement. There is no need to try and keep up with the cutting edge; the use of effective technology and techniques is important. But this does not mean to settle for yesterday's equipment donated by local businesses.

A second problem is the lack of technology expertise in the teaching and administrative staffs of the elementary and secondary schools and districts. This does not mean to imply that all staff members must be technological experts, instead all staff members must understand the technology mind-set and be able to practice effective techniques of assessment and utilize the technology available to do so. A district-wide technology plan is only as good as the end user's ability to implement it.

A third problem is the natural cultural lag in teaching and learning materials that continues to ignore interactive technology as a basic tool for learning. When combined with the natural delay built into budgeting processes for educational institutions, this requires educational leaders to continually plan in advance to overcome these obstacles.

However, a review of the research on technology in education offers much information that can help schools in their attempt to better incorporate technology in curriculum design and implementation. The research can be categorized as follows:

- Outcomes for students when a technology mind-set is utilized effectively.
- Outcomes for teachers when technology mind-set is utilized effectively.
- Certain features of technology-based resources are critical to effective technology applications in the classroom.

- Certain support factors must be present for the effective inclusion of technology into classroom instruction.
- State and federal program support factors have been effective in promoting increased use of technology in schools.

Student Outcomes

The effectiveness of technology in both curriculum design and delivery varies. The research indicates that, when the technologically grounded design and delivery principles are followed, the following can be expected:

- The expectation of learning is present instead of an expectation of content coverage or delivery.
- Increased performance when interactivity is an expectation.
- Planning begins by determining what are the learning needs.
- Curricular processes connected to ongoing assessment of student learning.
- Assessments are more effective when multiple technologies are integrated into the everyday classroom.
- Teaching and learning activities are a means to achieve the learning outcomes and are assessed in the same manner as student learning.
- Improved attitude and confidence for at-risk students.
- Improvement in student problem-solving skills and confidence.
- Significant improvement in the problem-solving skills of students with learning disorders.
- Writing skills and attitudes about writing for urban students.
- Improved writing skills as a result of using telecommunications.

It could be argued by technology skeptics that most of these outcomes could be achieved by other educational innovations. That could be true, except in the area of increased opportunities. Student outcomes are positive when the students are given the opportunity to construct the meaning (or learning) for themselves, and this interaction is augmented by the technological mind-set.

The type of student activity possible with technology is simply not available through any other learning modality. It is important to realize this is not about the use of any single piece of technology, rather, it is the mind-set developed through the use of technology. In addition, technology increases the potential of curriculum design. Theoretically speaking, technology increases the learning opportunities for all students to the maximum. Carried to its ultimate potential, the curriculum design would equal the sum total of the curriculum designs of all schools involved in the entire learning network. If a learning experience is offered in any of the educational settings, it is available to all educational settings within the learning network. The results and data can be shared across the network allowing all to learn from the lessons or adaptations developed by any of the participants.

Those experienced with learning networks grounded in a technological mind-set have pointed out the obstacles that must be overcome to make them effective learning and teaching modes. But the operative question is not the one often being asked. Currently, educators are too often studying and evaluating the learning labs and classrooms by asking: "Is this learning environment as effective as the traditional classroom?" The answer is almost always no. But that is not the right question.

The operative question is: "Is this learning environment and experience worthwhile?" If the answer is yes, then the learning should be utilized to its fullest potential. Basically, the comparison is the learning opportunity versus no learning opportunity at all. The lessons developed can then be used to expand the learning opportunities through more differentiated instructional opportunities.

Of course, any school system can increase its course offerings in other ways than by utilizing technology. However, learning grounded in technology has much potential in increasing the curriculum offerings through the reallocation of resources as opposed to the need for increased resources. Technologically focused learning also has the potential for making maximum use of master teachers. As educators continue to evaluate the effects of technology, the profession could ask the operative question and make the valid comparisons. It is not a question of the technical classroom versus the nontechnical classroom. It is a question of gaining opportunity through technology versus missing opportunity by refusing to use technology.

Teacher Outcomes

Research is showing that if voluntary use of technology is applied, the following results can be expected:

- Less direction and more student-centered teaching
- Increased emphasis on differentiated instruction for all students
- Teachers spending more time on advising students based on data
- Increased interest in teaching using the technology
- Increased interest in experimenting with emerging instructional techniques grounded in technology
- Teacher preference for multiple technologies
- Increased teacher and administrator productivity through sharing of information and results
- Increased planning and collaboration among colleagues
- Revision of curriculum design and delivery

- Greater participation in school improvement efforts
- More partnerships with business and industry to support technology efforts of the school
- Increased school involvement with community agencies
- Increased communication by administrator and teachers with parents

It is obvious that all of these outcomes are desirable. The ways for a school system to move toward their accomplishment are just as obvious, but not simplistic. First of all, the technology must be of high quality. Next, a staff development program must be implemented, so that teachers become technologically competent, and thus comfortable, in implementing technology in curriculum design, delivery, assessment, and the adaptation based on the results.

To assist teachers in their effort to become more adept at utilizing technology, school administrations must insist that technology, and the results of needs and learning assessments be a part of the learning-material adoption process. That is the way to get the technology mind-set into the mainstream process of curriculum design and development.

To assist in curriculum delivery, the school leadership must provide a quality staff development program and give it time to work. Many of the current teachers have had twenty or more years' experience in teaching without a technology mind-set. It is a difficult transition. Support and patience are probably as important as the tools and techniques. There are a variety of materials available such as the programs and components from the International Society for Technology in Education (ISTE).

Features of Technology-Based Resources

The following features of the school's technology resources are critical for the effective use of the technology mind-set in education. The resources should provide for or incorporate:

- Instant feedback on correctness of student response
- Immediate adjustment of task difficulty in relation to response
- Ease of use by teachers and students
- Sustained interest and use by students
- Tasks and processes not possible from books
- Student control of the pace of the learning program
- Opportunities for individualized problem solving
- Opportunities for multiple technologies
- Built-in assessments and procedures to match technology resources with learner needs
- Alignment with curriculum design and instructional resources

The following features are important in the application of technolog-based resources. The research studies suggest that technology should provide for or promote the following:

- Curriculum delivery that cannot be easily accomplished without technology
- Guidelines for teachers on how and when to integrate the technology into curriculum delivery
- Expansion and enhancement of the curriculum
- Integration into the current and emerging curriculum
- Access to educationally relevant programs
- Adaptability to home technology
- Ease of use and high interest
- Effective use within the regular learning environment or classroom
- Teachers who can promote meaningful student use of technology
- Adapted use of technology with diverse student populations
- Involvement of teachers and administrators in the design and delivery of the educational technology

This list of characteristics of resources points out the importance of teacher and administrator involvement in the selection process, and the significance of the quality of the hardware and software. Just any old stuff won't do.

Local Teacher Support Factors

The following teacher support factors will facilitate the infusion of technology into curriculum design and delivery:

- Time for teachers to plan, learn about, and implement technology applications
- Connection to a network of other technology-using teachers
- Availability of teacher-mentors and other peer support
- Involvement of principals and other administrators in planning, training, and implementation
- Development of the knowledge to critique and select technology applications
- Development of school- and classroom-level technology plans for teachers
- Involvement of teachers in deciding classroom use of technology
- Teacher access to technology for planning
- Preparation of new teachers to technology into curriculum delivery
- Ongoing staff development program to support integration of technology into curriculum design and delivery
- Increased opportunities for staff development and technical assistance
- Access to technology and telecommunications resources
- Awareness of and access to educational technology-based programs

- Awareness of centralized information resources related to technology use
- Teacher- and student-access to computers outside of school
- Opportunities for educators to grow professionally through conferences and dialogue outside the school environment
- Administrative commitment to technology
- Continual high-performance training

State and Federal Program Support Factors

One characteristic of technology is its connectivity. The governance structures affect connectivity. The wider the connectivity, the greater the resource potential. State and federal programs increase connectivity and resource potential without the usual administrative bureaucratic red tape characteristic of other curriculum programs. Effective state and federal programs should provide the following:

- Incorporation of technology into existing and emerging educational initiatives
- Incorporation of technology applications into state curriculum standards and guidelines
- Guidelines for local planning that promote funding allocations for staff development
- Statewide networks with electronic distribution
- Incentives to use and disseminate programs that work
- Telecommunications and distance learning for teacher staff development
- Identification and dissemination of model technology programs, practices, and projects
- Development of effective educational software, multimedia, and video for school and home use
- Study of the positive and negative consequences of technology on education and society

The effects of the technology mind-set on curriculum design and implementation are just emerging. The effects of the technology mind-set on the process of developing and/or revising curriculum designs have already been felt. The turnaround time on document revision has been greatly reduced, and the communications with participants has been greatly improved.

The effect of the technology mind-set on curriculum implementation is moving more slowly. It is in the area of curriculum implementation that the research and studies information presented in this chapter can be useful. It represents the best information we have at this time to proceed with the implementation of technology in the classroom. Continual study and research are called for to ensure that technology is used to provide new learning opportunities and methodologies. Anyone who has contact with the world outside the schoolhouse doors knows that technology is a part of the students' lives, now and in their future. The question is not whether curriculum design and implementation should include technology but how.

NOTE

1. Jay Sivin-Kachala and Ellen Bialo, *Report on the Effectiveness of Technology in Schools, 1990–1994* (Washington, D.C.: Software Publishers Association, 1730 M Street, NW, Washington, D.C. 20036, 1994).

REFERENCES

Apple Education Research Series, (1994). *Effectiveness Reports.* Cupertino, CA: Apple Computer, Inc., 20525 Maliani Avenue 95014.

Bagnall, R. (1994). "Performance indicators and outcomes as measures of educational quality: a cautionary critique," *International Journal of Lifelong Education*, 13, 1, pp. 19–32.

Biggs, J. (1999). *Teaching for Quality Learning at University.* Buckingham: Society for Research in Higher Education and Open University Press.

Biggs, J. (2003). "Enhancing teaching through constructive alignment," *Higher Education*, 32, 3, pp. 347–364.

Biggs, J. and Tang, C. (2007). *Teaching for Quality Learning at University*, 3rd ed. Berkshire: Society for Research in Higher Education and Open University Press.

Breeden, L., Hood, E. S., Solomon, G., Stout, C., Maak, L., and Rutkowski, K. M. (1994). *Building Consensus/Building Models: A Networking Strategy for Change.* Washington, D.C.: Federation of American Research Networks and the Consortium for School Networking.

Clark, Ian (2015). "Formative Assessment: Translating High Level Curriculum Practice into Classroom Practice." *The Curriculum Journal*, 26, 1, pp. 91–114.

Cradler, J. D. (1987). *Policy Recommendations for Program Improvement with Educational Technology in California Schools.* Redwood City, CA: Policy Analysis for California Education, San Mateo County Office of Education, 333 Main Street, 94063.

Cradler, J. D. (1993). *Monterey Model Technology Schools: Cumulative Research and Evaluation Report 1987–92.* Hillsborough, CA: Educational Support Systems, 1505 Black Mountain Road 94010.

Ewell, P. (2008). "Building academic cultures of evidence: a perspective on learning outcomes in higher education," paper presented at the symposium of the Hong Kong University Grants Committee on Quality Education, Quality Outcomes—the way forward for Hong Kong, Hong Kong, June, available at: www.ugc.edu.hk/eng/ugc/activity/outcomes/symposium/2008/present.html (accessed September 15, 2010).

Hadley, Martha, and Karen Sheingold. (1990). *Accomplished Teachers Integrating Computers into Classroom Practice*. New York: Bank Street College of Education Center for Children and Technology, 610 West !12th Street 10025.

Means, B., et al. (1993). *Using Technology to Education Reform*. Washington, D.C.: Office of Research, U.S. Department of Education, Office of Research and Improvement.

Tam, M. (2014). "Outcomes-based approach to quality assessment and curriculum improvement in higher education," *Quality Assurance in Education,* 22, 2, pp. 158–168.

Chapter 11

Student Credentialing

THE RATIONAL VERSUS NONRATIONAL DEBATE

For decades, there has been a societal debate about whether schools are rational or nonrational entities. To the public, the answer is emphatically, "of course they are rational!" To some educators, the response is an emphatic, "schools are nonrational." The debate is vital when deciding how schools should be evaluated with regard to student achievement. To those who claim that schools are rational entities, the answer is simple: set the curriculum, teach the curriculum, and test the curriculum. If the results, based on comparative data, are good, then the school is a successful one with regard to student achievement. This position assumes that exit standards, such as a high school diploma, will assure educational excellence for all. It assumes that anyone who achieved this plateau has reached a level of general competence. Proficiency testing and graduation exams are examples of this theory in practice. This position also assumes that letter grades and grade-point averages (GPAs) are the information that institutions of higher education and future employers are looking for.

On the other side of this accountability coin are the nonrational proponents, who claim that because schools and educators do not have control of enough variables to assure equivalent, universal student achievement, accountability for student achievement must be shared with all the stakeholders who affect a student's achievement level—specifically, the parent, home environment, and the students themselves.[1]

Neither of these positions is serving educational evaluation and accountability well. The "pure rationalists," who currently control the political climate, are leading the educational establishment down a road paved with "dumbed-down," boilerplate curriculum; schools teaching to the test; a reduction or elimination of arts curriculum and instruction; reduced electives;

stifled creativity and individuality; and convergent thinking. All these practices are false indicators of school excellence.

The "pure nonrationalists," who are out of favor with the political establishment, could best be described as naysayers. Such people offer only criticism and excuses to the rationalists' approach and do not have an acceptable
accountability model to present for consideration.

RATIONALE FOR STUDENT CREDENTIALING AS AN ACCOUNTABILITY MODEL FOR STUDENT ACHIEVEMENT

Education is too complex to assume that a terminal achievement such as high
school graduation means the same for every student. The knowledge explosion means that all knowledge can't be taught; consequently, curriculum
abandonment and thus specialization are occurring in both elementary and
secondary schools.

Therefore, the important element in student achievement evaluation is not a
generic test score or scores but an accountability concerning what specific skills
and knowledge the student has demonstrated. The decision of future employers
or continuing education should be based on the credentials that the student has
achieved. This credential would cover not only the three Rs but also the other
new basic skills as defined by Murname at a higher level of achievement than is
currently being pursued. Through credentialing, the high school diploma would
specify different levels of skill and knowledge that the student had achieved. In
other words, the credential becomes a validation of exactly what the diploma
means based on each individual student's skills and knowledge.

What is flawed with the current approach to the measurement of student
achievement is the assumption that minimum standards and commensurate
testing assure educational improvement and excellence. These minimum
standards are based on arbitrary numerical goals; if set too low, they create
a dumbing-down effect; if set too high, they create failure and organizational chaos. Adjusting to accommodate these two extreme positions is more
closely aligned to political maneuvering than to logical educational concepts.
The results have not served schools well. The current approach to student
achievement accountability based on minimum standards thinking makes no
provision for those students who fail. This "boilerplate, one standard fits all"
theory is not productive for the society. The "no child left behind" or "every
student succeeds" rhetoric, if carried to successful conclusion, will set high
expectations that no child is left behind and every child will learn intended
outcomes within a given period.

The sad fact is the rationalists have good reason to pursue their line of reasoning. The educational establishment, nonrationalists, would not create an accountability model on their own, so they've had to live with this consequence. Accountability for student achievement must be preserved. However, the model should be based on educational needs, not political maneuvering.

Credentialing would not mean the end of testing. It would create a new paradigm for its use, and supplement paper-and-pencil testing with multifactored assessment methods such as portfolios and evaluation from professionals in the field. Proficiency testing, based on minimum requirements for basic skill achievement, would continue. That information is vital and necessary to ensure basic skill development for all students. But the assessment of student achievement should not end there. Boilerplate standards and testing should be augmented by credentialing, which goes beyond basic skill testing, and through rubrics, specifying the skills and knowledge necessary for credentialing and showing exactly what skills and knowledge the student possesses. A student could graduate without being fully credentialed. The key element is that future employers and colleges could see where the student was based on their standards and proceed accordingly with decisions about the students' future academic needs.

Education should be a transitional experience, meaning that the purpose of each level of education is to prepare the student to be successful at the next level. Credentialing is a validation that such a condition, student by student, is either present or not present, and it indicates precisely where any deficiencies lie.

THE ISSUE OF TIME VERSUS LEARNING

Current accountability models for student achievement rely on periodic, norm-referenced tests as the valid measure. There is federal pressure to test annually, especially in English language arts and mathematics. Regardless of the content assessed, all the testing programs assume that time is a constant and learning is a variable. This assumption is contrary to what is known about teaching and learning. It is not educationally sound to base testing using time as the constant. To assume that all fourth-graders can be educated to the same level of achievement is, of course, folly. Therefore, a testing program designed to produce school accountability with time as the constant makes the following assumptions:

- All students can learn the intended learning outcomes at the same rate of speed.

- If all students have not learned at the same rate, the school's curriculum and instruction have failed.
- Students who fail the test must be retained within the curriculum until they demonstrate mastery of the test.
- Having a testing program with time as the constant will improve student achievement.
- If all or a significant percentage of the students receive the minimum or higher score, this data is verification that the academic needs of all students are being met.

In fact, the following assumptions, not accepted as a part of the rationale for testing programs with time as a constant, are most likely being made:

- If a significant percentage of the students are failing the test, the standards may be set too high for students who need more time to learn.
- If an overwhelming percentage of the students are passing the test, the standards may be too low for high-achieving students.
- When the percentage of students passing the test becomes so high that all schools have extremely high passing rates, the standards will be raised by the political authorities.
- For this testing program to be deemed an accurate accountability measure, a certain percentage of the students must fail.

Let's look at how these assumptions would change if a testing program was based on the assumption that time is a variable and learning is a constant.

- All students can learn the intended learning outcomes, but not necessarily at the same rate of speed.
- This variation in learning rates is reflective of the difference in learners and is not necessarily a valid evaluation of the curriculum and instructional programs.
- Students who fail the test continue to pursue the intended learning outcomes of the curriculum, demonstrating continual academic growth, until they demonstrate mastery on a subsequent exam.
- Having a testing program with learning as a constant will improve student achievement.
- Academic needs of students should be verified through individual testing that coincides with the learning speed of the individual student.
- The credentialing process will identify the specific skills and knowledge that each student possesses as they make the transition to the next level. This data will be used to plan the learning program for the student.

COGNITIVE FUNCTIONING AND STUDENT
ACHIEVEMENT EVALUATION

There are four stages of cognitive functioning: dualism, relativism, commitment, and empathy. Testing for boilerplate standards utilizes only dualism, which views knowledge in concrete, simplistic terms. It has a student orientation best described by the phrase, "tell me what's going to be tested and I'll study for it."

The next cognitive stage, relativism, is an I'm OK, you're OK perspective that views cognition as a concept without right and wrong answers. This is certainly a student orientation that denies the existence of valid and reliable testing that seeks specific answers. This cognitive stage has little relevance in assessing student achievement at the elementary and secondary levels.

It is within the two highest levels of cognitive functioning that schools wishing to educate and evaluate beyond boilerplate standards must develop assessment measures. These levels are commitment and empathy. Both are learner perspectives as opposed to student perspectives. A student perspective is based on demonstrating achievement to please or accommodate someone else. A learner perspective is based on demonstrating achievement to please or accommodate oneself. Students at the commitment level of cognitive functioning seek answers to questions that will help them understand and apply the knowledge gained from the educational opportunity. Students at the highest level of cognitive functioning are interested in how to use their knowledge and skills to help others. For the higher levels of cognitive functioning, the measure is not only what you can do but also what you will become.

In measuring the higher levels of cognitive functioning, schools will augment basic skills paper-and-pencil tests by combining measures of complex performance with indicators of understanding, systemized as follows: (1) performance in multiple contexts, (2) assessing the ability to question, and (3) assessing appropriate performance in unexpected situations.

In conclusion, the current testing mentality, based on boilerplate curriculum, instruction, and assessment, is equivalent to a medical doctor using a thermometer to treat a disease. The thermometer may indicate that a disease is present, but it will not cure the patient. Proficiency testing will indicate that certain students are not achieving basic skills within a set time frame based on one measure.

Student achievement evaluation should include analysis using multifactored assessment measures, including professional judgment from the next level of transition. Student achievement accountability measures should provide information to assist the school in maximizing the potential of all students, and supply specific information and data for transition to the next level. Individual student credentialing has the components and processes needed to accomplish this task and move accountability for student achievement toward a new paradigm that will raise standards and achievement.

CREDENTIALING PLAN

In developing a credentialing plan, the school must first identify the areas of credentialing. The most common academic areas are English language arts (i.e., reading and writing), mathematics computation and problem solving, and science reasoning. The school must then develop curriculum-based rubric assessments in each academic area. Figure 11.2 provides a sample rubric for English (Language Arts) Standards. The minimum score for each rubric is then determined. In order to be credentialed, students must also score at the state-determined level on any boilerplate assessments required. The credentialing process begins in the student's sophomore year and continues until graduation.

Schools may decide to credential in areas other than academics. Prime examples are employability skills and career awareness and exploration. Credentialing is defined as verification of the student's readiness for transition to the next level. This readiness may involve more than academic readiness. A credentialing plan for employability skills would require assessments that measure this readiness. In addition, the school may have program requirements in employability skills that the student must have met. Career awareness and exploration could include such requirements as an individual career

Student's Name: _____

Campus: _____

Academic/Career Major(s): _____

Advisor: _____

Academic Skills:

- Reading
  a. Student's score on district curriculum rubric: _____   Yes   No
     (Needed Total Score 2)
  b. Student's Score on State Proficiency: _____   Yes   No
     (Needed score 200)
  Is this student credentialed in this area?   Yes   No
  (If yes to a and b above, what is the date of the credentialing?) _____
  (If no, what is the intervention plan?)
  _____
  _____

Figure 11.1. Student Credentialing Summary Form

- Writing
  a. Student's score on district curriculum rubric: _____   Yes   No
     (Needed Total Score 2)
  b. Student's score on State Proficiency: _____   Yes   No
     (Needed Score 4)
  Is this student credentialed in this area?   Yes   No
  (If yes to a and b above, what is the date of the credentialing?) _____
  (If no, what is the intervention plan?)

  _____

  _____

- Mathematics
  a. Student's score on district curriculum rubric: _____   Yes   No
     (Needed Total Score 2)
  b. Student's Score on State Proficiency: _____   Yes   No
     (Needed Score 200)
  c. Student's Score on Academic Competencies: _____   Yes   No
     Related to Career Field:
     (Needed Score 4)
  Is the student credentialed in this area?   Yes   No
  (If yes to a, b, and c above, what is the date of credentialing?)
  (If no, what is the intervention plan?)

  _____

  _____

- Science Reasoning
  a. Student's score on district curriculum rubric: _____   Yes   No
     (Needed Total Score 2)
  b. Student's Score on State Proficiency: _____   Yes   No
     (Needed Score 200)
  Is this student credentialed in this area?   Yes   No
  (If yes to a and b above, what is the date of the credentialing?) _____
  (If no, what is the intervention plan?)

  _____

  _____

Career Awareness/Exploration:
  a. Has the student completed or reviewed the   Yes   No
     Individual Career Plan in the past year?
  (If no, what is the intervention plan?)

  _____

  _____

Is this student credentialed in this area?   Yes   No
(If no, what is the intervention plan?)

  _____

  _____

Figure 11.1.   (Continued)

Workplace Skills:

a. Has the student completed 95% of the   Yes   No
   career-technical hours?
(If no, what is the intervention plan?)

_____

b. Has the student passed the career-technical   Yes   No
   and related academic classes?
(If no, what is the intervention plan?)

_____

c. Has this student met or exceeded the established   Yes   No
   State Score on the Occupational Competency
   Analysis Profile?
(If no, what is the intervention plan?)

_____

Is the student credentialed in this area?   Yes   No
(If yes to a and b above, what is the date of the credentialing?) _____

Advisor's Signature: _____
Date:

CC: Student
    Advisor
    Student File
    Advisor'isor

Student's Name: _____

Instructor(s): _____

Rating Scale
4—Advanced Application
2—Basic Knowledge
1—Needs Remediation
N/A—Not Applicable

Rating	Course Abilities Standards—English 11
	A. Develop abilities in language arts.
	Higher thinking (analyze, evaluate, classify, predict, generalize, solve, decide, relate, interpret, simplify)
	Communications (present, demonstrate, persuade, collaborate, explain, defend, recommend)
	Goal setting/attainment (brainstorm, envision, research, plan, organize, persist)

Figure 11.2. **Sample Rubric for English (Language Arts) Standards**

	Use of the quality process (plan, draft, analyze, and revise when producing products)
	B. Be able to read, speak, and listen for a variety of purposes.
	Ability to use literature (specific authors, schools of literature)
	Ability to use mass media (newspapers, magazines, radio, television, movies, Internet, CD-ROM)
	Ability to conduct research (locate, observe/gather, analyze, conclude)
	Possess technical skills (read/write/present: instructions, tables, charts, reports [progress, research], proposal, letters [complaint, request, applications, response, recommendation], manual, form, checklist, resume, brochure, pamphlet, technical research, technical analysis, summary, advertisement, announcement; technology: word processing, spreadsheet, database, desktop publishing, Internet, search tools, AV production)
	Course Content Standards—English 11
	A. Read/view various forms of literature and technical writing to gain understanding and to critique/analyze the purpose, structure, tone, mood, and point of view.
	B. Present narratives, explanations, instructions, descriptions, summaries, critiques, and major persuasive and technical presentations.
	C. Use and display critical-listening skills.
	D. Read/view varous forms of literature to analyze, interpret, draw conclusions, and identify literary devices (flashback, simile, metaphor, foreshadowing, symbolism, personification, alliteration).
	E. Compose research-supported essays (introduction, thesis, body with 2–4 supported major points, transitions, conclusion).
	F. Create/make presentations utilizing technical information.
	G. Interpret fiction and nonfiction and relate it to life.
	H. Identify ideas, events, emotions, and attitudes in fiction and nonfiction.
	I. Speak for a variety of purposes using the conventions of standard English.
	J. Read/view/discuss to form beliefs and goals.
	K. Use a variety of sentence structures to enhance writing style.
	L. Develop proper paragraphs and join paragraphs into proper sequences.
	M. Using the writing process, organize, construct, and support a thesis statement following a logical format.
	N. Critique, defend, discuss, and compare the writing of self, course classmates, and others.

Figure 11.2.   (Continued)

	Content Standards—English 11 (Continued)
	O. Develop mechanically correct, clear, focused, and organized sentences and paragraphs.
	P. Compose for a variety of purposes (narrative, persuasion, expository) and audiences.
	Q. Complete a variety of career-related forms and be able to complete applications.
	R. Demonstrate ability to conduct oneself well at career-related interviews.
	S. Read, interpret, and apply technical information.
	T. Research technical information.
	Overall rating of student's Reading competency.
	Overall rating of student's Writing competency.
	Overall rating of student's Speech competency.
	Overall rating of student's Language Arts competency.
	Overall rating of student's English 11 competency.

Comments:

Instructor's Signature: _____

Rating	Course Abilities Standards—Technical Communications
	A. Develop abilities in language arts.
	Higher thinking (analyze, evaluate, classify, predict, generalize, solve, decide, relate, interpret, simlify)
	Communications (present, demonstrate, persuade, collaborate, explain, defend, recommend)
	Goal setting/attainment (brainstorm, envision, research, plan, organize, persist)
	Use of the quality process (plan, draft, analyze, and revise when producing products)
	B. Be able to read, speak, and listen for a variety of purposes.
	Ability to use literature (specific authors, schools of literature)
	Ability to use mass media (newspapers, magazines, radio, television, movies, Internet, CD-ROM)
	Ability to conduct research (locate, observe/gather, analyze, conclude)
	Possess technical skills (read/write/present: instructions, tables, charts, reports [progress, research], proposal, letters [complaint, request, applications, response, recommendation], manual, form,

Figure 11.2.   (Continued)

	Course Content Standards—Technical Communications (Continued)
	checklist, resume, brochure, pamphlet, technical research, technical analysis, summary, advertisement, announcement; technology: word processing, spreadsheet, database, desktop publishing, Internet, search tools, AV production)
	A. Read/view various forms of literature and technical writing to gain understanding and to critique/analyze the purpose, structure, tone, mood, and point of view.
	B. Present narratives, explanations, instructions, descriptions, summaries, critiques, and major persuasive and technical presentations.
	C. Use and display critical-listening skills.
	D. Read/view various forms of literature to analyze, interpret, draw conclusions, and identify literary devices (flashback, simile, metaphor, foreshadowing, symbolism, personification, alliteration).
	E. Compose research-supported essays (introduction, thesis, body with 2–4 supported major points, transitions, conclusion).
	F. Create/make presentations utilizing technical information.
	G. Interpret fiction and nonfiction and relate it to life.
	H. Identify ideas, events, emotions, and attitudes in fiction and nonfiction.
	I. Speak for a variety of purposes using the conventions of standard English.
	J. Read/view discuss to form beliefs and goals.
	K. Use a variety of sentence structures to enhance writing style.
	L. Develop proper paragraphs and join paragraphs into proper sequences.
	M. Using the writing process, organize, construct, and support a thesis statement following a logical format.
	N. Critique, defend, discuss, and compare the writing of self, classmates, and others.
	O. Develop mechanically correct, clear, focused, and organized sentences and paragraphs.
	P. Compose for a variety of purposes (narrative, persuasion, expository) and audiences.
	Q. Complete a variety of career-related forms and be able to complete applications.
	R. Demonstrate ability to conduct oneself well at career-related interviews.
	S. Read, interpret, and apply technical information.

	Course Content Standards—Technical Communications (Continued)
	T. Research technical information.
	Overall rating of student's Reading competency.
	Overall rating of student's Writing competency.
	Overall rating of student's Speech competency.
	Overall rating of student's Language Arts competency.
	Overall rating of student's Technical Communications competency.

Comments:

Instructor's Signature: _____

Figure 11.2. (Continued)

plan, campus mentors, and counseling activities. Vital to any credentialing plan is the description of intervention for students who haven't completed the requirements for credentialing. The process is ongoing, and the school does not expect that students will proceed through its requirements at the same pace.

Figure 11.1 presents an example of a credentialing summary form that is used for every student. This form follows the student through their academic career and provides the data for transition to the next level.

NOTE

1. Richard J. Murname and Frank Levy, *Teaching the New Basic Skills: Principles of Educating Children to Thrive in a Changing Economy* (New York: Free Press, 1986), 9.

REFERENCE

Clark, Ian (2015). "Formative Assessment: Translating High Level Curriculum Practice into Classroom Practice." *The Curriculum Journal*, 26, 1, pp. 91–114.

U.S. Department of Education. (2017). Every Student Succeeds Act. https://www.ed.gov/essa (accessed March 2017).

Index

Note: Page references for figures are italicized.

About the Authors

Leo H. Bradley, professor emeritus, holds a bachelor's degree in history, a master's degree in educational administration, and a doctorate in educational administration with minors in curriculum and twentieth-century American history.

His scholarly works include sole authorship of nine books, including *Total Quality Management for Schools* (both book and accompanying educational video); *Curriculum Leadership and Development*, 2nd Edition, including a Chinese language edition; *School Law for Public, Private, and Parochial Educators*, 2nd Edition; and *Competency Based Education*. Among his journal article topics are entry-year programs, mentorships, ethics, school law, curriculum design, and leadership theory. Bradley is a nationally recognized consultant for schools and businesses in the areas of curriculum, school law, total quality management, and leadership.

In his professional life, Bradley has held the positions of teacher, high school principal, assistant superintendent, and superintendent of schools. For the past twenty-seven years, he has been a professor in educational administration, serving as chair for seventeen, at Xavier University in Cincinnati, Ohio.

Bradley has many hobbies, including baseball history, songwriting, and musical performing. He has written and recorded more than forty songs for Fraternity Records, including the 1999 album "One Bounce and You're Out, The History of Baseball in Song," and the 2003 album "Remembering the Reds: The History of the Cincinnati Reds in Song."

Shirley A. Curtis has a bachelor's degree in elementary education, a master's degree in school counseling, and a doctorate in curriculum and instruction with a concentration in administration. Curtis has been an elementary and junior high school teacher, math coach, reading specialist, lead teacher, and an elementary principal of state-recognized schools and district of excellence. She was a member of the Ohio Department of Education Academic Distress Commission. For fifteen years, she was an adjunct professor in educational administration at Xavier University in Cincinnati, Ohio. Currently she is a teaching professor in Xavier's Educational Administration Master's Program and in the Department of Leadership Studies and Human Resource Development Doctoral Program. Curtis is a consultant for public, nonpublic, private, and charter schools as a mentor and advisor for new teachers and administrator. She designs professional development opportunities for school improvement. She has presented at the state and national levels and has received federal, state, and local educational grants. She has published articles with Educational Leadership, Principal Navigator, National Association of Elementary School Principal, Education, and NCTM's Teaching Children Mathematics. She is a recipient of the Milken National Educators Award and Ohio Presidential Award for Excellence. She is known for her strong influence in developing leadership qualities in others and for her passion for transformational leadership and advocating best instructional practices.

Thomas A. Kessinger received his B.S. in history with minors in philosophy and economics from Xavier University; he also received an MEd in educational research and curriculum from Xavier; he earned his MA in history from the University of Cincinnati; and he obtained PhD in interdisciplinary studies (education and economics) from the University of Cincinnati.

Currently he serves as an associate professor in teacher education, secondary education, and educational leadership at Xavier University. He has researched and written numerous articles for refereed journals and published three book chapters; in addition, he has presented his research findings at multiple conferences spanning the past thirty-five years. Earlier in his career, he served as a classroom teacher in grades 6–12 and department chair for grades K–12 in a public school district. Finally, he has written numerous grant proposals and received total grant awards in excess $300,000, especially in the area of service learning.

D. Mark Meyers, PhD, is an associate professor of leadership in the School of Education at Xavier University and past president of the Ohio Association of Private Colleges of Education. Formerly, he held a position of the dean of the College of Social Sciences, Health, and Education at Xavier University, from 2007 to 2014. While dean, Dr. Meyers led the creation of international partnerships in six countries as well as the development of the college motto, Collaborate, Innovate, Educate. An award-winning teacher, author, and consultant, Dr. Meyers has been active in the education profession for over twenty-five years. He is the chair of the AACTE Committee of Professional

Preparation and Accountability and serves on several boards including the Cincinnati Association for the Blind and Visually Impaired and Episcopal Retirement Services.

Meyers's research interests include the role of technology in preservice education, the impact of field-based pedagogy, and technology integration into the classroom. His teaching model stresses the interactive nature of the classroom in the spirit of Habermas's ideal speech situation. He is also the coauthor of several education textbooks, including *Teaching: An Introduction to the Profession.*

Printed in the USA
CPSIA information can be obtained
at www.ICGtesting.com
LVHW091047050924
790111LV00002B/146